THE HEALTHY EATER'S GUIDE TO FAMILY & CHAIN RESTAURANTS

D1367533

What to Eat in Over 100 Restaurant Chains Across America

Hope S. Warshaw, M.M.Sc., R.D.

The Healthy Eater's Guide to Family & Chain Restaurants: What to Eat in Over 100 Restaurant Chains Across America.
© 1993 by Hope S. Warshaw

Library of Congress Cataloging-in-Publication Data

Warshaw, Hope S., 1954-
        The healthy eater's guide to family & chain restaurants: what to eat
        in over 100 restaurant chains across America / Hope S. Warshaw.
               p.   cm.
        ISBN 1-56561-017-2 : 9.95
        1. Restaurants—United States—Guidebooks. 2. Low-calorie diet.
        3. Low-fat diet. 4. Low-cholesterol diet. I. Title. II. Title: Family & chain
        restaurants.

        TX907.2.W37   1993   93-7131
        647.9573—dc20   CIP

Editors: Jeff Braun, Donna Hoel
Cover Design: Eric Lecy
Text Design: Liana Raudys
Production Coordinator: Claire Lewis

Printed in the United States of America

Published by:
CHRONIMED Publishing
P.O. Box 47945
Minneapolis, MN 55447-9727

TABLE OF CONTENTS

DEDICATION

To those who nurture, love, and support—thanks.

ACKNOWLEDGMENTS

Thanks are due to the many people from the more than 100 restaurant chains contacted for menu and nutrition information. Various corporate employees, including registered dietitians, public relations and marketing representatives, and people from the front lines of research and development were helpful. When appropriate, restaurant's trademarked or signature items are indicated.

When nutrition information was not available from the restaurant chain, nutrition information was estimated with a computerized nutrient analysis program from N-Squared Computing, 3040 Commercial St. NE, Suite 240, Salem, Oregon, 97302 and nutrient composition tables from the USDA. Exchange information is based on the *1986 Exchange Lists for Meal Planning,* and guidelines used to calculate exchanges are based on those provided in Powers, M: *Nutrition Guide for Professionals: Diabetes Education and Meal Planning,* The American Dietetic Association, Illinois, and American Diabetes Association, Inc., Virginia.

Fun Food Facts added throughout this book were obtained from various publications as indicated. Guinness World Records were reprinted with permission of Facts On File, Inc., New York, from *The Guinness Book of Records,* 1993. Copyright ® 1993 by Guinness Publishing Ltd.

No book is completed by just the author alone. It is truly a group effort. I want to thank and acknowledge the editing skills of Jeff Braun and Donna Hoel; the text designing by Liana Raudys, the cover designing of Terry Dugan, and the efforts of production coordinator, Claire Lewis. Seeing this book to fruition was no easy task. I also appreciate David Wexler's and Jon Ebersole's receptiveness to this idea and foresight to recognize the consumer's need for this ground-breaking book.

Thanks also to many professional colleagues who lent their ears and ideas.

FOREWORD

You start out with good intentions. You want to eat less fat and a more healthful diet. But you also enjoy restaurants. You do just fine when you eat at home. But when you go out to eat you lapse into old unhealthy habits!

Researchers have studied this problem. Not surprising, they discovered that business lunches, parties, travel, and hurried, irregular meals discourage healthy eating. To overcome these hurdles, we all need strategies or coping skills to keep us on track.

In this book, Hope Warshaw provides those strategies and skills. Remember, permanent change takes time. So if you find yourself relapsing occasionally, don't fret. Pick up this book and review the tips and information. Next time out you're likely to make better choices.

Stress, depression, frustration, anxiety, or anger may trigger old eating habits. Self-control disappears when you're under prolonged stress or feeling low. You need coping skills such as the specific problem-solving strategies Hope has provided for you to use when under negative emotional stress.

There are several strategies to maintaining new healthy eating habits. We know that people who exercise regularly have a far greater chance of long-term success. It may be that the discipline needed for exercise also carries over to eating habits.

Positive support systems also affect long-term health and eating behaviors. Eating healthy, especially in social situations, is easier when you have support-ive family members, colleagues, and friends. Family members eating the same healthy foods and walking together each day can provide the support necessary for long-term success.

Your motivation must also be internal—it has to come from you. Focus on feeling good about yourself! You'll do better than those who think "I'm doing this to lose weight" or "I'm doing this to please my spouse."

So there are the keys for helping you maintain a healthy eating behavior. Start by reading this book and learn how to eat out successfully. Enlist the support of family and friends. They'll make it easier for you. Generate internal motivation (after all, you are the one who wants to be successful) and focus on the positive changes you have made. And don't forget that regular physical activity is also important to success. Enjoy your busy and active social life—including eating out in restaurants.

Marion J. Franz, M.S., R.D., C.D.E.
International Diabetes Center, Minneapolis
Vice President of Nutrition and Publications
Author, *Fast Food Facts* and *Exchanges For All Occasions*

PREFACE

This is a groundbreaking book. Never before has so much nutrition information been culled from restaurant chains across America. There's books that cover fast food restaurants, but no other book has specific information on over 100 family and chain restaurants.

Not only are there more restaurants listed here, but we've done your homework. In the pages ahead you'll find the Best Bets for healthier choices. There's no need to weed out the unhealthy choices. We've also gone one step further and Put It All Together with sample meals from each restaurant. These sections are designed to incorporate the guidelines of healthier eating today—balance, variety, and moderation.

In using this guide you'll note that exact nutrition information is provided for about half the restaurants. Nutrition information for the others is based on computerized nutrient analysis, estimates of recipes and ingredients, and conversations with restaurant representatives.

Several major restaurant chains are missing because they chose not to be included in this book. It is my hope, as a registered dietitian and nutrition educator, that this book demonstrates the consumer's need and desire for nutrition information from chain restaurants. Then when we revise this book more and more restaurants will be able to provide exact nutrition information.

Menu and nutrition information was initially requested and gathered in spring, 1992. Since restaurants frequently change menus, they were contacted again in spring, 1993 (just prior to publication). Approximately 50 percent of the chains responded with updated information.

As you use this guide, it is important to recognize that menus are in a constant state of flux, therefore some items may not be included here and some items listed may have been deleted from menus. An article further detailing restaurant survey information was published, entitled "America Eats Out: Nutrition in the Chain and Family Restaurant Industry," in the *Journal of The American Dietetic Association*, January 1993.

No doubt, eating out healthfully is a difficult, yet not impossible task. I know because I eat out regularly. When using this guide please keep balance, variety, and moderation in mind. Stay realistic and practical in your choices and what you expect from restaurants. Most importantly, enjoy what you eat.

Over the next few years I hope to see a greater emphasis and interest in preventive heath care, which certainly involves healthier eating. With that focus, perhaps we will see more restaurant food and nutrition labeling guidelines and a greater interest from restaurants in providing healthier options. I invite you to join me in creating consumer demand for healthier restaurant options. Be a change agent. Together we can make a difference.

Hope S. Warshaw, M.M.Sc., R.D.

AN INVITATION TO HEALTHY RESTAURANT EATING

As trends go, two that touch nearly all of us are: first, the surge in number and variety of chain restaurants and second, the increasing emphasis on healthier eating to achieve and maintain good health and prevent disease.

Wait a minute. Aren't these trends incompatible? Doesn't one fight the other?

Not if you approach eating out armed with the practical guidelines in this book. You'll find information on over 100 restaurant chains, in 10 categories: Burgers and More, Chicken Restaurants, Dessert Restaurants, Dinner Houses, Family Restaurants, Mexican Restaurants, Pizza and More, Sandwiches and Subs, Seafood Restaurants, and Steak Houses.

Rest assured, we're not talking just fast food restaurants, although they are covered. We're concerned with all types of chain and family restaurants, where so many of us eat so often.

Whether you have a sit-down dinner in a family restaurant, a quick breakfast at a fast food chain, munch a pizza for lunch, or have Mexican or Chinese food delivered via a faxed-in order, you're part of the eat-out generation.

- Today the average American (eight years old and older) eats out 198 times a year—nearly four times a week.

- On a typical day in 1991, 21 percent of Americans bought food from a restaurant to eat "off premises"—away from the restaurant.

- In 1992, according to the National Restaurant Association, Americans spent $323 billion eating out—42 percent of their food dollar.

Eating out definitely is part of our fast-paced lifestyle, not just a special treat as it was in years past.

GOALS OF HEALTHY EATING

The goals of eating sensibly are the same whether you eat out or at home. The following guidelines developed by the U.S. Department of Agriculture (USDA) and the Department of Health and Human Services are clear. Here's how to adapt them to eating away from home.

■ *Eat a variety of foods.* Vary the restaurants you frequent and what you order. Keep the five food groups in mind (breads, cereal, rice, and pasta; vegetables; fruits; milk, yogurt, and cheese; meats, poultry, and other protein foods). Select from all food groups for a balance of vitamins and minerals, and don't get in a rut.

■ *Maintain a healthy weight.* Restaurant meals can easily bounce you over your proper calorie total, so keep a watchful eye on total calories and fat.

■ *Choose a diet low in fat, saturated fat, and cholesterol.* Avoiding excessive fat in restaurant meals can be challenging because fat creates great taste and restaurants use it liberally in all forms. Learn which foods are oozing with fat and which ingredients and cooking methods add fat. For instance, there's a vast fat and calorie difference between broiled and deep-fried items.

■ *Choose a diet with plenty of vegetables, fruits, and grains.* Restaurant meals often lack fruit, are light on vegetables, and limited in fiber and grains. Order more vegetables—salads, side orders, sandwich trimmings. Fresh fruit doesn't appear on most restaurant menus, so take on fruit at a salad bar, drink fruit juice, bring fruit from home to eat during the day. For more grains with fiber, think pasta, potatoes (not fried), whole-grain breads, rice.

■ *Use sugar in moderation.* With few exceptions, foods high in sugar are high in fat. Determine how often you can have dessert and maintain your nutrition goals.

■ *Use salt and sodium in moderation.* Learn about foods, ingredients, sauces, and preparation methods that run up the salt and sodium count and limit these as possible. Ask that salt be omitted when possible.

■ *If you drink alcoholic beverages, do so in moderation.* Remember, alcohol is seven calories per gram. A good rule to follow is when drinking an alcoholic beverage, also have a nonalcoholic, noncaloric beverage by your side, such as water, mineral water, or diet soda.

SEVEN KEYS TO HEALTHIER EATING IN RESTAURANT CHAINS

Whatever your nutrition and health goals—shed a few pounds, lower blood cholesterol, control blood sugar, or simply maintain your current health—you can do it in chain restaurants. The following strategies are important:

1. Develop a can-do attitude. Too many of us think in negative equations: Eating out equals pigging out; eating out equals special occasion; eating out equals blowing our diet. These attitudes are self-defeating. Develop a can-do approach and believe that you can have a healthy and enjoyable meal when eating out. Slowly begin to change your ordering habits and types of restaurants in which you choose to dine.

2. Decide to eat out. For most of us, eating out is hardly a special occasion, so we need to factor in our nutrition and health goals. More frequent eating out means more careful monitoring. If you eat out only once a month, you might take a few more liberties, perhaps splitting a dessert.

3. Choose the site. Find restaurants that offer at least some healthier options. Remember, eating in chain restaurants lets you learn the menus and plan ahead, no matter where the individual restaurant is located.

4. Have a game plan. On your way to the restaurant, envision a positive outcome—a healthy and enjoyable meal. Plan your order accordingly, and don't become a victim of hasty choices.

5. Order for your stomach, not your eyes. As you peruse the menu, having planned ahead, watch for high fat foods, rich and heavy sauces, preparation methods such as frying, and ingredients that add fat. Also, keep in mind the less ordered, the less eaten. Go creative with a soup and salad, perhaps a couple of appetizers, one entree between you and a friend. Most restaurants simply serve too much food. You need to learn how to outsmart the menu.

6. Get it made to order. Don't be afraid to ask. Restaurants need and want your business, and if your requests are practical—such as leaving an item off, baked rather than fried potatoes, hold the mayo, dressing on the side—they are usually willing to accommodate. The healthy eating message is not lost on most restaurant chains.

7. Know when enough is enough. So many of us were brought up as members of the "clean-plate club." Now it's time for membership in the "leave-a-few-bites-on-the-plate club." To prevent overeating, order carefully and lightly, drink plenty of noncaloric fluids with the meal, and do ask for carryout containers.

HOW TO USE THIS BOOK

In the following pages, you'll find helpful information on healthier choices in over 100 of America's biggest and busiest chains. (Restauranteurs constantly check what's popular, so some items listed may be dropped or added.) The information helps you strike a nice balance between what your taste buds yearn for and what you know is the healthy choice. No one's expected to be saintly, just sensible.

Sections are alphabetical by the ten types of restaurant chains, such as Burgers and More, Dinner Houses, Desserts, etc. Within each section, individual chains are listed alphabetically. Nutrition Pros and Cons are included for each category of restaurant.

For example, under Nutrition Pros and Cons, you'll find tips such as: Pros—"Healthier options are available, although you might have to look through the menu carefully;" Cons—"Portions are larger than needed, even the healthier choices."

Under each restaurant chain is an alphabetical listing of the restaurant's Best Bets. These are the healthier menu items. Nutrition information is provided when available from the restaurants, including calories, carbohydrates (grams), protein (grams), fat (grams), cholesterol (milligrams), sodium (milligrams), as well as food exchange values.

PUTTING IT ALL TOGETHER

Lastly, sample menus are included to show how easy it is to design healthier meals. They are based on the following criteria:

Light Choice
(Low in calories, fat, and cholesterol)

- 400 to 700 calories (based on about 1,200 to 1,600 calories per day)

- 30 to 40 percent of calories from fat (total per day should be 30 percent or less)

- 100 to 200 mg. of cholesterol (total per day should be 300 mg. or less)

- 1,000 to 2,000 mg. of sodium (total per day should be 2,400 to 3,000 mg.)

Moderate Choice
(Moderate in calories, low in fat, and low in cholesterol)

- 600 to 1,000 calories (based on about 1,800 to 2,400 calories per day)

- 30 to 40 percent of calories from fat (total per day should be 30 percent or less)

- 100 to 200 mg. of cholesterol (total per day should be 300 mg. or less)

- 1,000 to 2,000 mg. of sodium (total per day should be 2,400 to 3,000 mg.)

ABOUT SALAD BARS

Salad or food bars (as they are known in steak houses) have become popular in dinner, family, pizza and steak restaurant chains. Surprisingly, salad bars can be high-fat disaster land. However, if you learn the following rules of thumb, the salad bar can be part of a healthy meal.

■ Use a smaller plate, if available.

■ Pile on lettuce, cucumbers, peppers, broccoli, and other healthy offerings.

■ Be careful with your dressing choice. A salad can become a nutrition disaster if "dressed" too lavishly.

■ Use low-calorie dressing if available. However, don't think these dressings have no fat and calories. Reduced- or low-calorie salad dressings still have about 20 to 30 calories per tablespoon.

Fat-free dressings contain 10 to 20 calories per tablespoon.

■ Low-calorie and fat-free dressings often swap fat and calories for sodium. Two tablespoons of low-calorie dressing can have as much as 900 mg. of sodium.

■ If regular dressing is used, go for the oil and vinegar-based dressings such as Italian or vinaigrette. Reach the ladle down to the vinegar and spices and avoid the oil at the top.

■ If a creamy dressing is selected, dot ever so lightly, then spread with vinegar, lemon juice, or lemon wedges. Or lightly dip salad fixings in dressing on the side. But take it easy, regular salad dressing contains 60 to 80 calories per tablespoon (mainly fat calories).

YOUR TRIP TO THE SALAD/FOOD BAR

Trips to the salad/food bar are included in sample meals under **Putting It All Together** in dinner, family, pizza, and steak houses. To provide an example of a healthy salad bar combination, we chose to use these salad bar ingredients in the sample meals. Nutrition information for Light and Moderate Choice sample meals including a trip to the salad/food bar is based on this salad. Meals containing salad bars refer you back to this page for the salad bar ingredients.

Greens (lettuce and spinach), 2 cups
Mushrooms, 1/4 cup
Broccoli, 1/2 cup
Cucumbers, 1/4 cup
Tomatoes, 1/4 cup
Onions, 1/8 cup
Bean sprouts, 1/4 cup

Carrots, 1/4 cup
Beets, 1/8 cup
Diced ham, 1/4 cup
Croutons, 1/4 cup
Garbanzo beans, 1/4 cup
Three-bean salad, 1/4 cup
Bacon bits, 1 tsp.
Sunflower seeds, 1 tsp.

BURGERS AND MORE

Some critics claim fast food has corrupted and, worse yet, dulled America's taste buds.

John and Karen Hess in their book *The Taste of America* state, "There is, in fact, about as much difference in taste among our feeding chains as there is among makes of American cars."

However, many "foodies" believe fast-food chains have redeemed themselves of late and deserve much credit for being trendsetters by providing healthier choices.

In the late 1980s, fast food burger chains could no longer remain blindfolded to consumer's demand for healthier choices. Now, menus are by no means healthy, but they are healthier.

The main gain for the health conscious is that it's easier to complement menu offerings and design a healthier meal. Perhaps it's a chicken sandwich and side salad, chef salad and muffin, or roast beef sandwich and low-fat shake.

So, can you eat healthier today in fast food chains? The answer is absolutely YES! Keep an eye out for high-fat ingredients, add-ons and dressings. Be creative with menu offerings and pick and choose carefully to design your healthy meal.

Nutrition Pros

■ Small portions are available.
■ No foods greet you at the table. What you order is what you eat.
■ Some higher fiber breads are offered, for instance multigrain buns.
■ Most chains use 100% vegetable oil or shortening for frying (slightly reduces cholesterol and saturated fat; makes virtually no calorie difference.)
■ Healthier cold beverages are available: low-fat milk, fruit juices, mineral water, ice tea, diet carbonated soft drinks.
■ Low-calorie salad dressings are available in most establishments, but sodium can be high.
■ Healthier dessert options include low-fat frozen yogurt in cone or dish; low-fat shakes; muffin.

Nutrition Cons

■ Overwhelming majority of menu entries are high in fat and sodium.
■ Cheese or cheese sauce and bacon are frequent sandwich toppers.
■ Chicken and fish start off healthy but most often end up buried among breading and oil, losing their nutritious virtues.
■ French fries still are the traditional sandwich accompaniment.
■ Frying is the preferred cooking style.

ARBY'S

Best Bets

	Calories	Carbohydrate (gm.)	Protein (gm.)	Fat (gm.)	Cholesterol (mg.)	Sodium (mg.)
Breakfast						
Blueberry muffin (1)	240	40	4	7	22	200
Sandwiches						
Regular roast beef	383	35	22	18	43	936
Junior roast beef	233	23	12	11	22	519
French dip	368	35	22	15	43	1018
French dip 'n Swiss	429	36	29	19	67	1438
Arby Q (roast beef with BBQ sauce)	389	48	18	15	29	1268
Grilled chicken deluxe	430	42	24	20	44	901
Grilled chicken BBQ	386	47	23	13	43	1002
Ham 'n cheese	355	35	25	14	55	1400
Turkey sub+	486	47	33	19	51	2033
*Light roast beef deluxe	294	33	18	10	42	826
*Light roast turkey deluxe	260	33	20	6	33	1262
*Light roast chicken deluxe	276	33	24	7	33	777
Potatoes						
French fries	246	30	2	13	0	114
Plain baked potato	240	50	6	2	0	58
Broccoli 'N Cheddar baked potato	417	55	11	18	22	361
Salads						
*Garden salad	117	11	7	5	12	134
*Roast chicken salad	204	12	24	7	43	508
*Chef salad	205	13	19	10	126	796
*Side salad	25	4	2	0	0	30
*Light Italian dressing+ (2 oz.)	23	4	0	1	0	1100

	Calories	Carbohydrate (gm.)	Protein (gm.)	Fat (gm.)	Cholesterol (mg.)	Sodium (mg.)
Soups						
Lumberjack mixed vegetable+	89	13	2	4	4	1075
Old fashioned chicken noodle+	99	15	6	2	25	929
Beverages						
Milk (2%) (8 oz.)	121	12	8	5	18	122
Orange juice (6 oz.)	82	20	1	0	0	2
Condiments						
Arby's sauce	15	3	0	0	0	113

One of Arby's light menu offerings. Light cholesterol-free mayonnaise used on sandwiches. + High in sodium.

PUTTING IT ALL TOGETHER

Light Choice
(Low in calories, fat, and cholesterol)
Light roast beef deluxe
French fries, small
Diet soft drink

Nutrition Values:
Calories 540
Carbohydrate (gm.) 63
Protein (gm.). 20
Fat (gm.) 23
% calories from fat 38
Cholesterol (mg.) 42
Sodium (mg.) 940

Exchanges:
4 Starch/Breads, 1 Meat (medium fat), 3 Fats

Moderate Choice
(Moderate in calories, low in fat, cholesterol)
Broccoli n' cheddar baked potato
Garden salad with light Italian
  dressing (2 oz.)
Milk (2%) (8 oz.)

Nutrition Values:
Calories 678
Carbohydrate (gm.) 82
Protein (gm.) 26
Fat (gm.) 29
% calories from fat 38
Cholesterol (mg.) 52
Sodium (mg.) 1717

Exchanges:
4 Starch/Breads, 2 Vegetables,
1 Milk (2%), 4 Fats

BURGER KING

Best Bets

	Calories	Carbohydrate (gm.)	Protein (gm.)	Fat (gm.)	Cholesterol (mg.)	Sodium (mg.)
Breakfast						
Blueberry mini-muffins (4)	292	37	4	14	72	244
Sandwiches						
Hamburger	260	28	14	10	30	500
Cheeseburger	300	28	16	14	45	660
BK Broiler™ chicken sandwich	280	29	20	10	50	770
Salads						
Chef salad	178	7	17	9	103	568
Chunky chicken salad	142	8	20	4	49	443
Garden salad	95	8	6	5	15	125
Side salad	20	4	1	0	0	10
Reduced-calorie Italian salad dressing (4 tbsp.)	15	3	1	1	0	355
Other						
Dinner roll	80	13	3	2	0	140
Baked potato	210	48	5	0	0	15
Popcorn	130	17	3	6	0	228
Chicken Tenders™ (6 piece)	236	14	16	13	38	541
Barbecue dipping sauce (2 tbsp.)	36	9	0	0	0	397
Sweet and sour dipping sauce (2 tbsp.)	45	11	0	0	0	52

	Calories	Carbohydrate (gm.)	Protein (gm.)	Fat (gm.)	Cholesterol (mg.)	Sodium (mg.)
Beverages						
Milk - 2% (8 oz.)	121	12	8	5	18	122
Orange juice (6 oz.)	82	20	1	0	0	2

PUTTING IT ALL TOGETHER

Light Choice
(Low in calories, fat, and cholesterol)
Chicken Tenders™ (6 piece)
Barbecue dipping sauce
   (2 tbsp./1 package)
Baked potato with sour cream (2 tbsp.)

Nutrition Values:
Calories 542
Carbohydrate (gm.) 72
Protein (gm.) 22
Fat (gm.) 19
% calories from fat 30
Cholesterol (mg.) 53
Sodium (mg.) 1027

Exchanges:
5 Starch/Breads, 1 Meat (medium)
3 Fats

Moderate Choice
(Moderate in calories, low in fat, cholesterol)
Hamburger, small
French fries, small
Garden salad with 2 tbsp.
   reduced-calorie Italian dressing

Nutrition Values:
Calories 615
Carbohydrate (gm.) 67
Protein (gm.) 24
Fat (gm.) 26
% calories from fat 40
Cholesterol (mg.) 79
Sodium (mg.) 1536

Exchanges:
4 Starch/Breads, 2 Meats (medium)
1 Vegetable, 3 Fats

FUN FOOD FACTS

• "Short lunch hours and expanding cities made going home for lunch impossible. Hot lunches were regarded as a necessity, and lunch pails were too working class. As a result, new kinds of restaurants tried to fill the growing gap in the middle." *Revolution At The Table*, **1988.**

CARL'S JR.

Best Bets

Breakfast	Calories	Carbohydrate (gm.)	Protein (gm.)	Fat (mg.)	Cholesterol (mg.)	Sodium (mg.)
English muffin						
with margarine†	190	30	6	5	0	280
Hot cakes						
with margarine	510	61	11	24	10	950

†Request without margarine and use jelly, honey or syrup.

Sandwiches

	Calories	Carbohydrate (gm.)	Protein (gm.)	Fat (mg.)	Cholesterol (mg.)	Sodium (mg.)
Carl's Original						
hamburger™	460	46	25	20	50	810
Hamburger	320	33	17	14	35	590
*Charbroiled BBQ						
chicken sandwich™	310	34	25	6	30	680
Santa Fe chicken						
sandwich™+	530	36	30	29	85	1230
Teriyaki chicken						
sandwich™	330	42	28	6	55	830

+High in sodium.

Salads

	Calories	Carbohydrate (gm.)	Protein (gm.)	Fat (mg.)	Cholesterol (mg.)	Sodium (mg.)
*Chicken salad to go	200	8	24	8	70	300
*Small garden salad to go	50	4	3	3	5	75
Reduced-calorie						
French dressing (2 tbsp.)	40	5	0	2	0	290
Reduced-calorie						
Italian dressing (2 tbsp.)	40	5	0	2	0	290
Salsa (2 tbsp.)	8	2	0	0	0	210

Other

	Calories	Carbohydrate (gm.)	Protein (gm.)	Fat (mg.)	Cholesterol (mg.)	Sodium (mg.)
*Lite potato	290	60	9	1	0	60

Beverages

	Calories	Carbohydrate (gm.)	Protein (gm.)	Fat (mg.)	Cholesterol (mg.)	Sodium (mg.)
Milk - 1% (10 oz.)	150	19	14	3	13	200
Orange juice (small)	90	21	2	0	0	2

PUTTING IT ALL TOGETHER

Light Choice
(Low in calories, fat, and cholesterol)
Charbroiled BBQ chicken sandwich™
Garden salad with reduced calorie
French dressing (2 tbsp.)
Milk - 2% (10 oz.)

Nutrition Values:
Calories 550
Carbohydrate (gm.) 62
Protein (gm.) .42
Fat (gm.) 14
% calories from fat 23
Cholesterol (mg.) 48
Sodium (mg.) 1245

Exchanges: 2 1/2 Starch/Breads, 3
Meats (lean), 2 Vegetables, 1 Milk (2%)

Moderate Choice
(Moderate in calories, low in fat, cholesterol)
Carl's Original hamburger™
Lite potato
Salsa (4 tbsp.)

Nutrition Values:
Calories 776
Carbohydrate (gm.) 110
Protein (gm.) .34
Fat (gm.) 21
% calories from fat 25
Cholesterol (mg.) 50
Sodium (mg.) 1290

Exchanges:
7 Starch/Breads, 2 Meats (medium),
1 Vegetable, 2 Fats

Marked as "Lite Menu" in nutrition information.

HARDEE'S

Best Bets

	Calories	Carbohydrate (gm.)	Protein (gm.)	Fat (gm.)	Cholesterol (mg.)	Sodium (mg.)
Breakfast						
Three pancakes*	280	56	8	2	15	890
Oatbran raisin muffin	410	59	8	16	50	380
Sandwiches						
Hamburger	260	33	10	10	30	510
Roast beef-regular	280	29	18	11	40	870

HARDEE'S (cont.)

	Calories	Carbohydrate (gm.)	Protein (gm.)	Fat (gm.)	Cholesterol (mg.)	Sodium (mg.)
Sandwiches (cont.)						
Western BBQ beef sandwich	345	48	18	9	n/a	n/a
Turkey sub+	390	53	29	7	65	1420
Roast beef sub+	370	57	23	5	45	1400
Ham sub+	370	52	25	7	45	1400
Grilled chicken breast sandwich	310	34	24	9	60	890
Salads						
Chef salad	214	5	20	13	44	910
Garden salad	184	3	12	12	34	250
Side salad	20	1	2	<1	0	15
Salad Dressings						
Reduced-calorie French	130	21	2	5	n/a	n/a
Reduced-calorie Italian	90	5	0	8	n/a	n/a
Fat-free French	70	17	0	0	n/a	n/a
Fat-free Italian	25	6	0	0	n/a	n/a
Other						
French fries, regular	230	30	3	11	0	85
Mashed potatoes (4 oz.)	70	16	2	<1	0	260
Chicken noodle soup	80	9	6	2	n/a	n/a
Vegetable beef soup	80	12	6	2	n/a	n/a
Desserts						
Cool twist™ cone, frozen yogurt vanilla/chocolate	180	29	4	4	15	85
Beverages						
Milk - 2% (8 oz.)	145	12	9	4	18	150
Orange juice (10 oz.)	140	34	2	<1	0	5

Nutrition information without added margarine or syrup; n/a= not available; + High in sodium.

PUTTING IT ALL TOGETHER

Light Choice
(Low in calories, fat, and cholesterol)
Turkey Sub
Cool Twist™ cone, vanilla

Nutrition Values:
Calories 570
Carbohydrate (gm.) 82
Protein (gm.) 33
Fat (gm.) 11
% calories from fat 17
Cholesterol (mg.) 80
Sodium (mg.) 1505

Exchanges:
3 Starch/Breads, 3 Meats (lean),
2 Fruits, 1/2 Milk (2%)

Moderate Choice
(Moderate in calories, low in fat, cholesterol)
Three pancakes (request syrup and
    margarine on side), with syrup (3
    Tbsp.) and margarine (1 pat)
Orange juice (10 oz.)

Nutrition Values:
Calories 604
Carbohydrate (gm.) 122
Protein (gm.) 11
Fat (gm.) 8
% calories from fat 15
Cholesterol (mg.) 15
Sodium (mg.) 955

Exchanges:
4 Starch/Breads, 4 Fruits, 1 Fat

JACK-IN-THE-BOX

Best Bets

	Calories	Carbohydrate (gm.)	Protein (gm.)	Fat (gm.)	Cholesterol (mg.)	Sodium (mg.)
Breakfast						
Pancake platter	612	87	15	22	99	888
Sandwiches						
Hamburger	267	28	13	11	26	556
Cheeseburger	315	33	15	14	41	746
Chicken fajita pita (1)	292	29	24	8	34	703
Chicken and mushroom sandwich+	438	40	28	18	61	1340
Grilled chicken fillet+	431	36	29	19	65	1070
Sirloin steak sandwich	517	49	29	23	66	1050

+ *High in sodium.*

JACK-IN-THE-BOX (cont.)

	Calories	Carbohydrate (gm.)	Protein (gm.)	Fat (gm.)	Cholesterol (mg.)	Sodium (mg.)
Salads						
Chef salad	325	10	30	18	142	900
Side salad	51	trace	7	3	trace	84
Low-calorie Italian salad + dressing (4 tbsp.)	25	2	trace	2	0	810
Other						
French fries, small	219	28	3	11	0	121
Sesame breadsticks	70	12	2	2	trace	110
Guacamole (2 tbsp.)	30	2	1	3	0	128
Salsa	8	2	<1	0	0	27
Beverages						
Milk - 2% (8 oz.)	122	12	8	5	18	122
Orange juice (6 oz.)	80	20	1	0	0	0

PUTTING IT ALL TOGETHER

Light Choice
(Low in calories, fat, and cholesterol)
Chef salad
Low-calorie Italian dressing (2 tbsp. or 1/2 package)
Salsa (4 tbsp./2 packages)
Sesame breadsticks (2)

Nutrition Values:
Calories 494
Carbohydrate (gm.) 39
Protein (gm.) 34
Fat (gm.) 23
% calories from fat 42
Cholesterol (mg.) 142
Sodium (mg.) 1579

Exchanges:
2 Starch/Breads, 3 Meats (high fat), 2 Vegetables

Moderate Choice
(Moderate calories, low in fat, cholesterol)
Chicken fajita pita (1)
French fries, small
Milk - 2% (8 oz.)

Nutrition Values:
Calories 633
Carbohydrate (gm.) 69
Protein (gm.) 35
Fat (gm.) 24
% calories from fat 34
Cholesterol (mg.) 52
Sodium (mg.) 946

Exchanges:
4 Starch/Breads, 2 Meats (lean), 1 Milk (2%), 2 Fats

KRYSTAL'S

Best Bets

	Calories	Carbohydrate (gm.)	Protein (gm.)	Fat (mg.)	Cholesterol (mg.)	Sodium (mg.)
Krystal (small hamburger)	158	15	9	7	21	339
Chicken sandwich	392	44	21	16	33	707
Chili (regular)	214	22	11	8	16	674
Chili (large)	322	33	17	11	25	1012
French fries (small)	338	61	3	9	8	105

PUTTING IT ALL TOGETHER

Light Choice
(Low in calories, fat, and cholesterol)
Chili (regular)
French fries (small)

Nutrition Values:
Calories 552
Carbohydrate (gm.) 83
Protein (gm.) .14
Fat (gm.) 17
% calories from fat 28
Cholesterol (mg.) 24
Sodium (mg.) 779

Exchanges:
5 Starch/Breads, 3 Fats

Moderate Choice
(Moderate calories, low in fat, cholesterol)
Krystals (2 hamburgers)
French fries (small)

Nutrition Values:
Calories 654
Carbohydrate (gm.) 91
Protein (gm.) 21
Fat (gm.) 23
% calories from fat 32
Cholesterol (mg.) 50
Sodium (mg.) 783

Exchanges:
5 Starch/Breads, 1 Meat (medium),
3 Fats

FUN FOOD FACTS

• Carbonated sodas were packaged almost exclusively in glass bottles until the aluminum can was introduced in 1960. The American invention that did away with the need for a can opener or "church key", Alcoa's tab-top can, made its debut in 1963. *The Browser's Book of Beginnings, 1984.*

McDONALD'S

Best Bets

Breakfast	Calories	Carbohydrate (gm.)	Protein (gm.)	Fat (gm.)	Cholesterol (mg.)	Sodium (mg.)
Apple Bran, fat-free muffin	180	40	5	0	0	200
Cheerios® (3/4 cup)	80	14	3	1	0	210
English muffin						
with spread	170	26	5	4	0	285
without spread	140	26	5	1	0	230
Hotcakes (3)						
with margarine						
(2 pats and syrup)	440	74	8	12	8	685
plain pancakes (3)	250	43	8	4	8	570
Syrup (3 tbsp.)	120	28	0	0	0	5
Wheaties® (3/4 cup)	90	19	2	1	0	220

Sandwiches

Sandwiches	Calories	Carbohydrate	Protein	Fat	Cholesterol	Sodium
Hamburger	255	30	12	9	37	490
Cheeseburger	305	30	15	13	50	725
McLean deluxe™	320	35	22	10	60	670
McLean deluxe™ with cheese	370	35	24	14	75	890

Salads

Salads	Calories	Carbohydrate	Protein	Fat	Cholesterol	Sodium
Chef salad	170	8	17	9	111	400
Chunky chicken salad	150	7	25	4	78	230
Garden salad	50	6	4	2	65	70
Side salad	30	4	2	1	33	35
Lite vinaigrette dressing (2 tbsp.; 2 servings per packet)	24	4	0	1	0	120
Reduced-calorie red French dressing (2 tbsp.)	80	10	0	4	0	230

Others

Others	Calories	Carbohydrate	Protein	Fat	Cholesterol	Sodium
Chicken fajitas	190	20	11	8	35	310
French fries, small	220	26	3	12	0	110

	Calories	Carbohydrate (gm.)	Protein (gm.)	Fat (gm.)	Cholesterol (mg.)	Sodium (mg.)
Low-fat milkshake (10.4 oz.)						
vanilla	290	60	11	1	10	170
chocolate	320	66	11	2	10	240
strawberry	320	67	11	1	10	170
Desserts						
Low-fat frozen yogurt cone (3 oz.)	105	22	4	1	3	80
McDonaldland® cookies (2 oz.)	290	47	4	9	0	300
Beverages						
Milk - 1% (8 oz.)	110	12	9	2	10	130
Orange juice (6 oz.)	80	20	1	0	0	20
Grapefruit juice (6 oz.)	70	17	1	0	0	20
Apple juice (6 oz.)	80	21	0	0	0	30

PUTTING IT ALL TOGETHER

Light Choice
(Low in calories, fat, and cholesterol)
Wheaties® (3/4 cup)
Milk - 1% (8 oz.)
Grapefruit juice (6 oz.)

Nutrition Values:
Calories 280
Carbohydrate (gm.) 50
Protein (gm.) .12
Fat (gm.) 3
% calories from fat 10
Cholesterol (mg.) 10
Sodium (mg.) .350

Exchanges:
1 Starch/Bread, 1 Fruit, 1 Milk (2%)

Moderate Choice
(Moderate calories, low in fat, cholesterol)
Chunky chicken salad with
   lite vinaigrette dressing (2 tbsp.)
Apple bran, fat-free muffin (1)
Vanilla low-fat milkshake (10.4 oz.)

Nutrition Values:
Calories 644
Carbohydrate (gm.) 111
Protein (gm.) 41
Fat (gm.) 6
% calories from fat 8
Cholesterol (mg.) 88
Sodium (mg.) 720

Exchanges:
3 Starch/Breads, 3 Meats (lean),
   2 Vegetables, 2 Fruit

RAX

Best Bets

	Calories	Carbohydrate (gm.)	Protein (gm.)	Fat (gm.)	Cholesterol (mg.)	Sodium (mg.)
Sandwiches						
Regular Rax	262	25	18	10	15	707
Philly melt	396	40	25	16	27	1055
*Roast beef delight	268	n/a	n/a	10	25	n/a
*Turkey delight	227	n/a	n/a	5	40	n/a
*Grilled chicken delight	286	n/a	n/a	10	46	n/a
Salads						
*Gourmet garden salad	134	13	7	6	2	350
*Grilled chicken garden salad	202	14	19	9	32	747
*Side salad	16	n/a	n/a	<1	<1	n/a
Lite Italian (4 tbsp.)	63	8	0	3	0	294
*Fat-free dressings						
Ranch (3 tbsp.)	48	n/a	n/a	0	0	n/a
Italian (3 tbsp.)	18	n/a	n/a	0	0	n/a
Catalina (3 tbsp.)	48	n/a	n/a	0	0	n/a
Others						
French fries	282	36	3	14	3	75
Baked potato†	264	61	6	0	0	15
Condiments						
Mushroom sauce (1 oz.)	16	1	1	<1	0	113
Barbecue sauce (.5 oz.)	11	3	0	0	0	158

*One of Rax Lighterside items.
†Available with broccoli and cheese or chili and cheese. Request light or hold cheese.

PUTTING IT ALL TOGETHER

Light Choice
(Low in calories, fat, and cholesterol)
Grilled chicken garden salad with
fat-free Catalina dressing (3 tbsp.)

Nutrition Values:
Calories 250
Carbohydrate (gm.) 24
Protein (gm.) 21
Fat (gm.) 9
% calories from fat 32
Cholesterol (mg.) 32
Sodium (mg.) 747

Exchanges:
1/2 Starch/Bread, 2 Meats (lean),
3 Vegetables, 1 Fat

Moderate Choice
(Moderate in calories, low in fat, cholesterol)
Regular Rax
Barbecue sauce (1 pkt. - .5 oz.)
Baked potato with fat-free Ranch
dressing (3 tbsp.)

Nutrition Values:
Calories 585
Carbohydrate (gm.) 99
Protein (gm.) 26
Fat (gm.) 10
% calories from fat 15
Cholesterol (mg.) 15
Sodium (mg.) 880

Exchanges:
5 Starch/Breads, 2 Meats (medium),
1/2 Fruit

ROY ROGER'S

Best Bets

Breakfast	Calories	Carbohydrate (gm.)	Protein (gm.)	Fat (mg.)	Cholesterol (mg.)	Sodium (mg.)
Pancake platter with syrup and butter*	386	63	5	13	51	547
Sandwiches						
Roast beef	317	29	27	10	55	785
Roast beef, large	360	30	34	12	73	1044
Others						
Quarter chicken, Roy's Roaster (breast/wing; no skin)	190	2	32	6	n/a	n/a

ROY ROGER'S (cont.)	Calories	Carbohydrate (gm.)	Protein (gm.)	Fat (gm.)	Cholesterol (mg.)	Sodium (mg.)
French fries, small	268	32	4	14	42	165
Hot-topped potato, plain	211	48	6	0	0	65
Grilled chicken salad	120	2	18	4	60	520
Lo-Cal Italian dressing (2 tbsp.)	70	2	0	6	n/a	100
Beverages						
Milk - 2% (8 oz.)	120	11	8	5	18	130
Orange juice (8 oz.)	120	32	2	<1	0	n/a

Salad bar available. Low-cal Italian dressing available.
*Suggest ordering without butter. Nutrition information available from Roy Rogers includes syrup and butter.

PUTTING IT ALL TOGETHER

Light Choice
(Low in calories, fat, and cholesterol)
Pancake platter with syrup and butter
Orange juice (8 oz.)
Coffee with milk (2 tbsp.)

Nutrition Values:
Calories 521
Carbohydrate (gm.) 96
Protein (gm.) .8
Fat (gm.) 14
% calories from fat 24
Cholesterol (mg.) 53
Sodium (mg.) 563

Exchanges:
4 Starch/Breads, 2 Fruits, 3 Fats

Moderate Choice
(Moderate in calories, low in fat, cholesterol)
Cheeseburger, small
Salad bar - lettuce, broccoli, garbanzo
    beans, alfalfa sprouts, potato salad
    (1/4 cup), pineapple chunks
    (canned - 1/2 cup)

Nutrition Values:
Calories 565
Carbohydrate (gm.) 66
Protein (gm.) 21
Fat (gm.) 23
% calories from fat 37
Cholesterol (mg.) 37
Sodium (mg.) 1276

Exchanges:
3 Starch/Breads, 2 Meats (medium),
1 1/2 Fruit, 2 Fats

SONIC

Best Bets

	Calories	Carbohydrate (gm.)	Protein (gm.)	Fat (gm.)	Cholesterol (mg.)	Sodium (mg.)
Sandwiches						
Chicken sandwich	319	41	21	9	47	890
Grilled chicken sandwich	265	23	21	10	63	716
Fish sandwich	277	38	17	7	6	655
Sides						
French fries (regular)	233	37	3	8	8	50
Tater tots	150	19	2	7	10	330

PUTTING IT ALL TOGETHER

Light Choice
(Low in calories, fat, and cholesterol)
Grilled chicken sandwich
Tater tots

Nutrition Values:
Calories 415
Carbohydrate (gm.) 42
Protein (gm.) .23
Fat (gm.) 17
% calories from fat 37
Cholesterol (mg.) 73
Sodium (mg.) .1046

Exchanges:
3 Starch/Breads, 2 Meats (medium),
1 Fats

Moderate Choice
(Moderate in calories, low in fat, cholesterol)
Fish sandwich
French fries (regular)

Nutrition Values:
Calories 510
Carbohydrate (gm.) 75
Protein (gm.) .20
Fat (gm.) 15
% calories from fat 26
Cholesterol (mg.) 14
Sodium (mg.) .705

Exchanges:
5 Starch/Breads, 1 Meat (medium),
2 Fats

WENDY'S

Best Bets

	Calories	Carbohydrate (gm.)	Protein (gm.)	Fat (gm.)	Cholesterol (mg.)	Sodium (mg.)
Sandwiches						
Plain single	340	30	24	15	65	500
Jr. hamburger	260	33	15	9	35	570
Jr. cheeseburger	310	34	18	13	35	770
Grilled chicken sandwich	290	35	24	9	60	670
Salads						
Grilled chicken salad	200	9	25	8	55	690
Deluxe garden salad	110	9	7	5	0	380
Caesar side salad	160	18	10	6	10	700
Side salad	60	6	4	3	0	200
Reduced-calorie Italian dressing (2 tbsp.=1/2 packet)	40	3	0	4	0	340
Reduced-calorie blue cheese dressing (2 tbsp.=1/2 packet)	65	1	1	7	25	260
Fat-free French dressing (2 tbsp.= 1/2 packet)	35	8	0	0	0	180
Others						
Chili (8 oz.)	190	21	19	6	40	670
Chili (12 oz.)	290	31	28	9	60	1000
Saltines (2 each, 1 package)	25	<1	4	1	0	80
Plain baked potato	270	63	6	0	0	20
Broccoli and cheese potato	400	58	8	16	trace	455
Chili and cheese potato	500	71	15	18	25	630
French fries, small	240	33	3	12	0	145
Breadstick (1)	130	24	4	3	5	250

	Calories	Carbohydrate (gm.)	Protein (gm.)	Fat (gm.)	Cholesterol (mg.)	Sodium (mg.)
Beverages						
Milk - 2% (8 oz.)	110	11	8	4	20	115

PUTTING IT ALL TOGETHER

Light Choice
(Low in calories, fat, and cholesterol)
Chili, large (12 oz.)
Deluxe garden salad with
  reduced-calorie Italian dressing
Breadstick (1)

Nutrition Values:
Calories 540
Carbohydrate (gm.) 67
Protein (gm.) .37
Fat (gm.) 18
% calories from fat 30
Cholesterol (mg. 65
Sodium (mg.) 1650

Exchanges:
4 Starch/Breads, 3 Meats (medium),
1 Fat

Moderate Choice
(Moderate in calories, low in fat, cholesterol)
Stuffed potato with chili and cheese
Garden salad
Reduced-calorie Italian dressing
Milk - 2%

Nutrition Values:
Calories 740
Carbohydrate (gm.) 94
Protein (gm.) 28
Fat (gm.) 28
% calories from fat 34
Cholesterol (mg.) 45
Sodium (mg.) 1145

Exchanges:
5 Starch/Breads, 2 Vegetables, 1 Milk,
3 Fats

WHATABURGER

Best Bets

	Calories	Carbohydrate (gm.)	Protein (gm.)	Fat (gm.)	Cholesterol (mg.)	Sodium (mg.)
Breakfast						
Pancakes (without syrup or butter)	259	40	11	6	0	842
Sandwiches						
Whataburger Jr.™	304	31	15	14	30	684
Justaburger™	265	28	12	12	25	547
Grilled chicken sandwich (without dressing)	385	46	34	9	66	989
Fajita taco, chicken	272	35	18	7	33	691
Fajita taco, beef	326	34	22	12	28	670
Grilled turkey sandwich	439	49	33	15	46	968
Steak sandwich	387	32	35	12	61	1164
Salads						
Grilled chicken salad	150	14	23	1	49	434
Garden salad	56	11	3	1	0	32
Lite vinaigrette (2 oz.)+	36	5	0	2	0	878
Others						
French fries, junior	221	25	4	12	0	146
Vanilla shake, small	322	50	9	9	37	169
Oatmeal raisin cookie	222	37	4	7	28	70
Beverages						
Orange juice (6 oz.)	77	18	1	0	0	2
Milk, 2% (8 oz.)	113	11	8	4	18	113

PUTTING IT ALL TOGETHER

Light Choice
(Low in calories, fat, and cholesterol)
Grilled chicken fajita
Combination salad with lite vinaigrette
  (2 oz.)
Orange juice (6 oz.)

Nutrition Values:

Calories	444
Carbohydrate (gm.)	.69
Protein (gm.)	21
Fat (gm.)	.12
% calories from fat	.24
Cholesterol (mg.)	32
Sodium (mg.)	1782

Exchanges:
2 Starch/Breads, 2 Meats (lean),
2 Vegetables, 1 1/2 Fruits, 1 Fat

Moderate Choice
(Moderate in calories, low in fat, cholesterol)
Whataburger, Jr.™
Vanilla shake, small

Nutrition Values:

Calories	.626
Carbohydrate (gm.)	81
Protein (gm.)	.24
Fat (gm.)	.23
% calories from fat	.33
Cholesterol (mg.)	67
Sodium (mg.)	.853

Exchanges:
2 Starch/Breads, 2 Meats (medium),
2 Fruits, 1 Milk, 2 Fats

FUN FOOD FACTS

•In the 1880's the Hamburg steak traveled with a wave of German immigrants to America, where it became known as the "hamburger steak" and then the "hamburger". Exactly when and why the patty was put in a bun is unknown. But when served at the 1904 St. Louis World's Fair, it was already a sandwich with its name further abbreviated to "hamburg". And some three decades before McDonald's golden arches would become the gateway to hamburger heaven, the chain of White Castle outlets popularized the Tartar legacy. *Extraordinary Origins of Everyday Things,* 1987.

CHICKEN CHAINS

Fried chicken—breast, thigh, or wing; potatoes—mashed or French fried; corn on the cob; creamy coleslaw. That was the chicken chains' simple menu of yesteryear. Diversification then meant offering extra crispy or hot and spicy recipes, but fried was the only style.

The menu remains much the same for most chicken chains, especially those with southern roots. However, a few of the older restaurants are learning it's hard for some Americans to crunch on the fat-filled crispy batter without a twinge or two of guilt.

Several chicken chains are marketing health with the labels "rotisseried" and "skin-free." These words are carefully planned to suggest health benefits. Unfortunately, that's stretching it—a lot.

Most chains are also touting frying in 100 percent cholesterol-free oil. Big deal! On a positive note, though, several chains have added healthier flame-broiled or marinated chicken preparations.

Nutrition Pros

■ No foods greet you at the table. What you order is what you eat. You have maximal control.

■ Menus are a la carte. That makes ordering and eating smaller quantities easier.

■ Grilled, broiled, roasted, and rotisseried are healthier options sometimes available.

■ Healthier side items are plentiful: corn, beans, rice, potatoes, but watch that they're not dowsed in butter or gravy.

Nutrition Cons

■ The main course in most chicken chains is battered and fried, though exceptions are growing.

■ Don't be fooled by the healthy sound of skinless and skin-free. They're not much healthier than the real thing.

■ Many side items are high in calories and fat: French fries, fried okra, coleslaw, potato salad, biscuits.

■ Salad and unadulterated raw or cooked vegetables are not on most menus.

■ Fruit is simply not discussed, unless hidden in a pastry crust.

CHICKEN FACTS

There are several important misconceptions when it comes to chicken. Among them are:

Misconception #1. White meat is far healthier than dark meat. True, white meat has fewer calories and less fat, but chicken without the skin—prepared healthfully—is still a healthy, low-fat choice. Choose what pleases your palate.

Misconception #2. The fat's in the skin. Yes, chicken with skin has more fat and more calories, especially if fried. However, some fat definitely resides in the chicken meat as well.

Misconception #3. The cholesterol is all in the skin. Dead wrong! Cholesterol is just about the same with or without skin.

Misconception #4. Chicken's cholesterol count is far lower than red meat. Also dead wrong. Chicken, white or dark, with or without skin, fried or not fried, has about as much cholesterol, if not more, than lean or not-so-lean red meat.

However, there is more saturated fat in red meat than in chicken.

Certainly much of the fat and calories, as well as the crunch of fried chicken lies in the skin.

If you have the willpower, you will improve the nutrition profile of fried chicken tremendously by pulling off the skin. Obviously that means the crispy or extra crispy crust comes along, too.

But don't forget, it's still fried—and the calories and fat are still higher than in roasted, rotisseried, or grilled versions. Restaurants preparing skinless chicken simply take the skin off before battering and frying, which saves few or no calories and fat.

No matter how you carve it, making a constant diet of fast food chicken will not be smart for heart or waistline. However, an occasional fix of fried chicken won't tip the scales, either. Your best bet is to take advantage of those chicken restaurants offering healthier and tasty options.

THE TRUTH ABOUT CHICKEN

	Calories	Fat (gm.)	Percent calories from fat	Saturated fat (gm.)	Cholesterol (mg.)
Chicken, white meat					
—roasted with skin	167	7	36	2	72
—roasted without skin	140	3	19	1	7
—fried with skin	217	12	50	3	77
Chicken, dark meat					
—roasted with skin	215	13	56	4	77
—roasted without skin	174	8	42	2	79
—thigh fried with skin	253	19	66	4	99
Chicken wing					
—roasted with skin	248	17	60	5	73
—fried with skin	271	17	58	5	93
For comparison:					
Ground beef					
—broiled, regular fat	165	12	64	5	51
—broiled, extra lean	161	10	58	4	53

Nutrition information is for a 3-oz. cooked portion.

BOJANGLES

Best Bets

	Calories	Carbohydrate (gm.)	Protein (gm.)	Fat (gm.)	Cholesterol (mg.)	Sodium (mg.)
Chicken						
Skin-free, Southern, breast (4 oz.)	271	11	28	13	104	869
Skin-free, Southern, thigh (3.2 oz.)	264	10	19	17	88	592
Skin-free, Southern, leg (1.8 oz.)	128	5	7	12	54	312
Sandwiches						
Grilled filet, no mayo	329	37	27	7	59	418
Fixin's						
Biscuit	239	30	4	11	1	588
Dirty rice	167	21	5	7	12	397
Cajun pintos	124	25	6	0	0	463
Coleslaw	105	19	1	4	0	406

PUTTING IT ALL TOGETHER

Light Choice
(Low in calories, fat, and cholesterol)
Grilled filet without mayonnaise
Coleslaw

Nutrition Values:
Calories 434
Carbohydrate (gm.) 56
Protein (gm.) 28
Fat (gm.) 11
% calories from fat 23
Cholesterol (mg.) 59
Sodium (mg.) 824

Exchanges:
3 Starch/Breads
3 Meats (lean)
2 Vegetables

Moderate Choice
(Moderate in calories, low in fat, cholesterol)
Skin-free Southern chicken breast
Cajun pintos, Dirty rice, Biscuit (1)

Nutrition Values:
Calories 802
Carbohydrate (gm.) 87
Protein (gm.) 43
Fat (gm.) 32
% calories from fat 36
Cholesterol (mg.) 117
Sodium (mg.) 2317*
*High in sodium

Exchanges:
6 Starch/Breads, 3 Meats (lean)
4 Fats

CHICK-FIL-A

Best Bets

	Calories	Carbohydrate (gm.)	Protein (gm.)	Fat (gm.)	Cholesterol (mg.)	Sodium (mg.)
Sandwiches/Nuggets						
Chick-Fil-A® Sandwich	360	28	40	9	66	1174
Chick-Fil-A® Deluxe Sandwich	368	30	41	9	66	1178
Chick-n-Q® Sandwich	409	41	28	15	10	1197
Chargrilled Chicken Sandwich®	258	24	30	5	40	1121
Chargrilled Chicken Deluxe Sandwich (lettuce and tomato)	266	26	31	5	40	1125
Grilled 'n Lites™ (2 skewers)	97	4	20	2	3	280
Salads/Side Orders						
Carrot and raisin salad (1 cup)	116	18	1	5	6	8
Hearty Breast of Chicken Soup, small	152	11	16	3	46	530
Chargrilled chicken garden salad (no dressing)	126	8	20	2	28	567
Tossed salad	21	4	1	0	0	19
Salad Dressing						
Lite Italian (3 tbsp.)	43	7	1	1	0	856
Dessert						
Ice Dream®	134	19	4	5	24	51

CHICK-FIL-A (cont.)

PUTTING IT ALL TOGETHER

Light Choice
(Low in calories, fat, and cholesterol)
Hearty Breast of Chicken Soup,
  small (8.5 oz.)
Chargrilled Chicken Garden Salad
  with Lite Italian dressing (3 tbsp.)
Ice Dream®

Nutrition Values:
```
Calories . . . . . . . . . . . . . . . . . . . . . . .458
Carbohydrate (gm.) . . . . . . . . . . . . . 44
Protein (gm.) . . . . . . . . . . . . . . . . . . . .41
Fat (gm.) . . . . . . . . . . . . . . . . . . . . . . . .12
% calories from fat . . . . . . . . . . . . . . 24
Cholesterol (mg.) . . . . . . . . . . . . . . . 100
Sodium (mg.) . . . . . . . . . . . . . . . . . 1502
```

Exchanges:
2 Starch/Breads, 4 Meats (lean)
1 Vegetable , 1 Milk (2%)

Moderate Choice
(Moderate in calories, low in fat, cholesterol)
Chargrilled Chicken Sandwich®
  Deluxe
Carrot and raisin salad, 1 cup
Tossed salad with ranch
  salad dressing (3 tbsp.)

Nutrition Values:
```
Calories . . . . . . . . . . . . . . . . . . . . . . . 580
Carbohydrate  (gm.) . . . . . . . . . . . . . 54
Protein (gm.) . . . . . . . . . . . . . . . . . . . 34
Fat (gm.) . . . . . . . . . . . . . . . . . . . . . . . 26
% calories from fat . . . . . . . . . . . . . . 40
Cholesterol (mg.) . . . . . . . . . . . . . . . 63
Sodium (mg.) . . . . . . . . . . . . . . . . . 1358
```

Exchanges:
3 Starch/Breads, 3 Meats (lean)
2 Vegetables, 3 Fats

CHURCH'S CHICKEN

Best Bets

Chicken
Fried breast
Fried leg

Side Items
Roll
Mashed potatoes (hold gravy)
Cajun rice
Jalapeno pepper
Corn on the cob (hold butter)

PUTTING IT ALL TOGETHER

Light Choice
(Low in calories, fat, and cholesterol)
Fried chicken breast
Corn on the cob, Cajun rice

Nutrition Values:
```
Calories . . . . . . . . . . . . . . . . . . . . . . . 521
Carbohydrate (gm.) . . . . . . . . . . . . . 57
Protein (gm.) . . . . . . . . . . . . . . . . . . . 31
Fat (gm.) . . . . . . . . . . . . . . . . . . . . . . . 19
% calories from fat . . . . . . . . . . . . . . 33
Cholesterol (mg.) . . . . . . . . . . . . . . . 87
Sodium (mg.) . . . . . . . . . . . . . . . . . 1283
```

PUTTING IT ALL TOGETHER

Exchanges:
4 Starch/Breads, 3 Meats (lean)
2 Fats

Moderate Choice
(Moderate in calories, low in fat, cholesterol)
Fried chicken legs (3)
Mashed potatoes (hold gravy)
Corn on the cob (hold butter)
Jalapeno peppers

Nutrition Values:
Calories 604
Carbohydrate (gm.) 38
Protein (gm.) 53
Fat (gm.) 26
% calories from fat 39
Cholesterol (mg.) 170
Sodium (mg.) 2014*
                                    High in sodium
Exchanges:
2 Starch/Breads, 6 Meats (lean)
1 Vegetable, 2 Fats

EL POLLO LOCO

Best Bets

	Calories	Carbohydrate (gm.)	Protein (gm.)	Fat (gm.)	Cholesterol (mg.)	Sodium (mg.)
Chicken breast (3 oz.)	160	0	26	6	110	390
Chicken taco	180	18	13	6	35	300
Chicken burrito	310	30	23	11	65	510
Chicken Fajita meal (Includes rice, beans, 3 tortillas, and salsa)	780	120	41	18	58	1060
Steak burrito	450	31	31	22	70	740
Steak taco	250	18	18	12	40	410
Vegetarian burrito	340	54	14	7	20	360
Flame-broiled chicken salad	160	11	22	4	45	440

Side Items

Rice	110	19	1	2	0	220
Corn	110	20	3	2	0	110
Beans	100	16	5	3	0	460
Coleslaw	90	7	1	8	0	35
Flour tortilla (1)	90	15	3	3	0	150
Corn tortilla (1)	60	13	1	1	0	25
Salsa (2 oz.)	10	1	0	0	0	90

EL POLLO LOCO (cont.)

PUTTING IT ALL TOGETHER

Light Choice
(Low in calories, fat, and cholesterol)
Vegetarian burrito
Corn, Coleslaw

Nutrition Values:
Calories 540
Carbohydrate (gm.) 81
Protein (gm.) 18
Fat (gm.) 17
% calories from fat 28
Cholesterol (mg.) 20
Sodium (mg.) 505

Exchanges:
4 Starch/Breads, 3 Vegetables, 3 Fats

Moderate Choice
(Moderate in calories, low in fat, cholesterol)
Chicken fajita meal
3 flour tortillas, 4 tbsp. salsa,
Beans (4 oz.), and rice (1 oz.)

Nutrition Values:
Calories 780
Carbohydrate (gm.) 120
Protein (gm.) 41
Fat (gm.) 18
% calories from fat 21
Cholesterol (mg.) 58
Sodium (mg.) 1060

Exchanges:
6 Starch/Breads, 3 Meats (lean),
2 Vegetables, 1 Fat

KFC

Best Bets

Chicken	Calories	Carbohydrate (gm.)	Protein (gm.)	Fat (gm.)	Cholesterol (mg.)	Sodium (mg.)
Original Recipe®						
Center breast (2.9 oz.)	260	8	25	14	92	609
Drumstick (2 oz.)	152	3	14	9	75	269
KFC® Skin-free Crispy						
Center breast (3.7 oz.)	296	9	26	16	59	435
Drumstick (1.9 oz.)	166	5	12	9	42	256

Other KFC Items

	Calories	Carbohydrate	Protein	Fat	Cholesterol	Sodium
Buttermilk biscuit	235	28	5	12	1	655
Mashed potatoes/gravy	71	12	2	2	<1	339
Corn on the cob	90	16	3	2	<1	11
Coleslaw	114	13	1	6	4	177

To reduce fat, hold the gravy. (Nutrition information includes gravy.) KFC uses only 100% vegetable oil.

PUTTING IT ALL TOGETHER

Light Choice
(Low in calories, fat, and cholesterol)
Skin-free Crispy Drumsticks (2)
Mashed potatoes with gravy
Corn on the cob (hold butter)

Nutrition Values:
Calories 493
Carbohydrate (gm.) 32
Protein (gm.) 39
Fat (gm.) 22
% calories from fat 40
Cholesterol (mg.) 88
Sodium (mg.) 1612

Exchanges:
2 Starch/Breads
4 Meats (lean)
2 Fats

Moderate Choice
(Moderate in calories, low in fat, cholesterol)
Skin-free Crispy breast (1)
Biscuit
Corn on the cob
Coleslaw

Nutrition Values:
Calories 735
Carbohydrate (gm.) 67
Protein (gm.) 34
Fat (gm.) 36
% calories from fat 44
Cholesterol (mg.) 64
Sodium (mg.) 1278

Exchanges:
4 Starch/Breads, 3 Meats (lean)
1 Vegetable, 5 Fats

LEE'S FAMOUS RECIPE

Best Bets

Chicken
1/4 roast chicken breast
   (dinner* or piece)
1/4 roast chicken leg (dinner* or piece)
Skin-free breast or drumstick

* *Served with 2 vegetables and biscuit*

Country Vegetables and Salads
Mashed Potatoes
Green beans
Corn on the cob
Red beans/rice
Country Rice
Biscuit

FUN FOOD FACTS

• France's King Henry IV stated in his coronation speech that he hoped each peasant in his realm would have "a chicken in his pot every Sunday." This quote was later paraphrased by President Herbert Hoover.
Food Lover's Companion, 1990.

LEE'S FAMOUS RECIPE (cont.)

PUTTING IT ALL TOGETHER

Light Choice
(Low in calories, fat, and cholesterol)
Red beans and rice (2 orders)
Corn on the cob (no butter)
Biscuit (1)

Nutrition Values:
Calories 670
Carbohydrate (gm.) 105
Protein (gm.) 19
Fat (gm.) 21
% calories from fat 28
Cholesterol (mg.) 0
Sodium (mg.) 1931

Exchanges:
7 Starch/Breads
4 Fats

Moderate Choice
(Moderate in calories, low in fat, cholesterol)
1/4 roast chicken breast dinner
(pull skin)
Mashed potatoes (hold gravy)
Green beans, Biscuit (1), Apples

Nutrition Values:
Calories 747
Carbohydrate (gm.) 87
Protein (gm.) 34
Fat (gm.) 30
% calories from fat 37
Cholesterol (mg.) 90
Sodium (mg.) 2007*
*High in sodium

Exchanges:
4 Starch/Breads, 3 Meats (lean)
1 Vegetable, 1 Fruit, 4 Fats

MRS. WINNER'S

Best Bets

	Calories	Carbohydrate (gm.)	Protein (gm.)	Fat (gm.)	Cholesterol (mg.)	Sodium (mg.)
Rotisserie chicken, white quarter (5 oz.)	242	2	38	9	139	700
Rotisserie chicken, dark quarter (4 oz.)	216	2	29	10	140	590
Skin-free fried chicken breast (4 oz.)	280	14	23	15	115	480
leg (1.7 oz.)	110	5	10	6	50	115
Oven roasted potatoes	139	31	4	<1	<1	132
Honey yeast roll (1)	200	35	8	4	7	290

Best Bets

Sandwiches
BBQ rotisseries chicken deluxe
Grilled chicken deluxe

Sides
Whipped potatoes (hold gravy)
Green beans
Baked beans
Country biscuit

PUTTING IT ALL TOGETHER

Light Choice
(Low in calories, fat, and cholesterol)
Rotisserie chicken,
 1/4 lunch white quarter
Oven roasted potatoes
Honey yeast roll

Nutrition Values:

Calories	581
Carbohydrate (gm.)	67
Protein (gm.)	50
Fat (gm.)	14
% calories from fat	22
Cholesterol (mg.)	147
Sodium (mg.)	1122

Exchanges:
4 Starch/Breads
5 Meats (lean)

Moderate Choice
(Moderate in calories, low in fat, cholesterol)
Order a la carte
Skin-free fried chicken breast
Baked beans
Green beans
Honey yeast roll

Nutrition Values:

Calories	770
Carbohydrate (gm.)	86
Protein (gm.)	40
Fat (gm.)	31
% calories from fat	36
Cholesterol (mg.)	130
Sodium (mg.)	1688

Exchanges:
5 Starch/Breads, 3 Meats (lean)
2 Vegetable, 3 Fats

POPEYE'S FAMOUS FRIED CHICKEN

Best Bets

Chicken
Fried chicken breast
Fried chicken leg
BBQ chicken sandwich

Side Items
Red beans and rice
Seafood gumbo
Corn
Jalapeno pepper
Biscuit

POPEYE'S (cont.)

PUTTING IT ALL TOGETHER

Light Choice
(Low in calories, fat, and cholesterol)
BBQ chicken sandwich
Corn, Jalapeno pepper

Nutrition Values:
Calories 510
Carbohydrate (gm.) 63
Protein (gm.) 36
Fat (gm.) 12
% calories from fat 24
Sodium (mg.) 2365*
High in sodium.

Exchanges:
4 Starch/Breads, 5 Meats (lean)

Moderate Choice
(Moderate in calories, low in fat, cholesterol)
Fried chicken drumsticks (2)
Red beans and rice, Corn, Biscuit (1)

Nutrition Values:
Calories 759
Carbohydrate (gm.) 77
Protein (gm.) 43
Fat (gm.) 32
% calories from fat 36
Cholesterol (mg.) 102
Sodium (mg.) 1249

Exchanges:
5 Starch/Breads, 4 Meats (lean), 4 Fats

PUDGIE'S FAMOUS CHICKEN

Best Bets

Chicken
Skinless fried chicken breast
Skinless fried chicken leg
Roast skinless chicken

Side Orders
Dinner roll
Corn on the cob
Riviana rice

PUTTING IT ALL TOGETHER

Light Choice
(Low in calories, fat, and cholesterol)
Skinless fried chicken breast (1)
Corn on the cob (2, no butter), Roll (1)

Nutrition Values:
Calories 576
Carbohydrate (gm.) 63
Protein (gm.) 34
Fat (gm.) 24
% calories from fat 37
Cholesterol (mg.) 82
Sodium (mg.) 1355

Exchanges: 4 Starch/Breads, 3 Meats
(lean), 3 Fats

Moderate Choice
(Moderate in calories, low in fat, cholesterol)
Skinless fried chicken breast (1)
Skinless fried chicken drumstick (1)
Riviana rice, Corn on the cob

Nutrition Values:
Calories 781
Carbohydrate (gm.) 70
Protein (gm.) 51
Fat (gm.) 34
% calories from fat 39
Cholesterol (mg.) 147
Sodium (mg.) 1625

Exchanges: 5 Starch/Breads, 5 Meats
(lean), 3 Fats

DESSERT/ICE CREAM CHAINS

Here are some basics about healthier choices for most dessert/ice cream chains:

Regular ice cream has about 150 to 180 calories per 4 ounces, with 7 to 10 grams of fat. The super premium ice creams start at about 260 calories per 4 ounces and about 15 to 20 grams of fat.

Light Ice Cream: The word light is somewhat deceiving. These have between 100 and 130 calories for 4 ounces, with about 3 to 6 grams of fat—similar to regular ice cream. Don't be fooled by light super premiums that have more calories than regular ice cream.

Fat-Free Ice Cream: These products have about 100 calories per 4 ounces and zero fat. The calories aren't that much lower because fat's been replaced by carbohydrate-based fillers.

Sorbets/Sherbets/Ices: Surprisingly, these have about the same calories as regular ice cream, although sherbet has less fat. Ices contain no fat and around 140 calories for 4 ounces. The calories are mainly from carbohydrate.

Regular or Low-Fat Frozen Yogurt: These products contain 3 to 4 percent fat, about the amount of fat in regular milk. Calories range from 130 to 160 per 4 ounces with a few grams of fat.

Nonfat Frozen Yogurt: There's no fat in these, but the calories run about 100 per 4 ounces. Again, when fat is taken out, it's replaced by carbohydrate-based fillers.

Sugar-free, Low-fat Frozen Yogurt: Now the sugar's been taken out and aspartame (NutraSweet®), a low-calorie sweetener, has been added. Calories still tally 90 to 100 per 4 ounces.

Sugar-free, Fat-free Frozen Yogurt: There's aspartame for sweetness and carbohydrate fillers for bulk. These have around 80 calories per 4 ounces.

Nutrition Pros

- Small portion sizes are offered.
- Healthier toppings can be found—fresh fruit, granola, nuts, raisins.
- Frozen desserts are easy to share.

Nutrition Cons

- Indulgence is easy.
- Unhealthy toppers are plentiful: candies, cookies, hot fudge, butterscotch.
- Frozen yogurts, especially the sugar-frees and fat-frees, can have many unfamiliar ingredients.

A Special Note

Nutrition information under Best Bets is for a 4 fluid-ounce serving—small, but the industry standard. Nutrition content of the same type of frozen dessert can vary slightly depending on the flavor. Several companies base nutrition information on an average of all flavors. Nutrition values under "Putting It All Together" are just for desserts and are based on between 150 and 350 calories each, rather than criteria mentioned on page 5.

BASKIN ROBBINS ICE CREAM AND YOGURT

Best Bets

	Calories	Carbohydrate (gm.)	Protein (gm.)	Fat (gm.)	Cholesterol (mg.)	Sodium (mg.)
Sherbet and Ices						
Daiquiri ices	140	35	0	0	0	15
Light™ Ice Cream						
Almond buttercrunch	130	16	3	6	12	n/a
Double raspberry	120	19	2	4	9	n/a
Fat-Free Frozen Dessert (contains Simplesse®)						
Caramel banana	100	23	2	0	1	n/a
Chocolate wonder	120	26	3	0	1	n/a
Sugar-Free Frozen Dessert—Low, Lite 'n Luscious® (contains NutraSweet®)						
Strawberry	80	17	2	1	3	70
Chocolate chip	100	20	3	2	4	n/a
Soft-Serve Sorbet						
Strawberry	100	20	0	0	0	20
Frozen Yogurt						
Low-fat strawberry	120	24	4	1	5	40
Nonfat strawberry	100	24	3	0	0	40
TrulyFree Frozen Yogurt (sugar-free, fat-free, cholesterol-free; contains NutraSweet® and Simplesse®)						
Cafe mocha	70	16	4	0	0	14
Novelties—Sundae Bars™						
Light chocolate with caramel ribbon (1)	150	24	3	5	11	75

	Calories	Carbohydrate (gm.)	Protein (gm.)	Fat (gm.)	Cholesterol (mg.)	Sodium (mg.)
Cones						
Sugar (1)	60	11	1	1	0	45
Waffle (1)	140	28	3	2	0	5

PUTTING IT ALL TOGETHER

Light Choice
(Low in calories, fat, and cholesterol)
Rainbow sherbet (one scoop)
Fresh fruit (blueberries)

Nutrition Values:
Calories 200
Carbohydrate 44
Protein (gm.) 2
Fat (gm.) 2
% calories from fat 9
Cholesterol (mg.) 6
Sodium (mg.) 89

Exchanges:
1 Starch/Bread, 2 Fruits

Moderate Choice
(Moderate in calories, in fat, cholesterol)
Light ice cream
    praline dream (kiddie double, 5 oz.)
    in sugar cone

Nutrition Values:
Calories 223
Carbohydrate (gm.) 32
Protein (gm.) 5
Fat (gm.) 9
% calories from fat 36
Cholesterol (mg.) 14
Sodium (mg.) 151

Exchanges:
1 Starch/Bread, 1 1/2 Fruits, 1 Fat

BRAUM'S ICE CREAM & DAIRY STORE

Best Bets

	Calories	Carbohydrate (gm.)	Protein (gm.)	Fat (gm.)	Cholesterol (mg.)	Sodium (mg.)
Ice cream—						
premium light	102	15	3	3	n/a	56
Frozen yogurt	180	16	3	3	n/a	35
Diet sugar-free						
frozen yogurt						
(with NutraSweet®)	90	13	3	3	n/a	n/a
Fat-free frozen yogurt	90	20	4	0	n/a	55

BRAUM'S ICE CREAM & DAIRY STORE (cont.)

PUTTING IT ALL TOGETHER

Light Choice
(Low in calories, fat, and cholesterol)
Frozen yogurt—fat free in dish
   (medium, 6 oz.)

Nutrition Values:
Calories 135
Carbohydrate (gm.) 30
Protein (gm.) 6
Fat (gm.) 0
% calories from fat 0
Cholesterol (mg.) . . . . n/a
Sodium (mg.) 83

Exchanges:
2 Starch/Breads

Moderate Choice
(Moderate in calories, low in fat, cholesterol)
Ice cream—premium light
   (medium, 6 oz.)
Waffle cone

Nutrition Values:
Calories 293
Carbohydrate (gm.) 51
Protein (gm.) 8
Fat (gm.) 7
% calories from fat 22
Cholesterol (mg.) 0
Sodium (mg.) 89

Exchanges:
2 Starch/Breads, 1 1/2 Fruits, 1 Fat

BRESLER'S ICE CREAM & YOGURT

Best Bets

	Calories	Carbohydrate (gm.)	Protein (gm.)	Fat (gm.)	Cholesterol (mg.)	Sodium (mg.)
Royal Lites	132	9	5	5	16	70
Sherbets	160	34	1	2	6	n/a
Ices	137	34	n/a	0	0	n/a
Gourmet yogurt	116	22	4	2	7	n/a
Lite yogurt	108	24	4	0	0	n/a

FUN FOOD FACTS

• In the 1920s drugstores invaded the light lunch market, setting up their own soda fountains. In addition to ice cream and syrup-based beverages, the soda fountains served coffee, cakes, canned soups, and sandwiches. By 1929, it was estimated that 61 percent of all drugstore sales were at the soda fountain. *Revolution at the Table, 1988.*

PUTTING IT ALL TOGETHER

Light Choice
(Low in calories, fat, and cholesterol)
Ices (1 scoop)

Nutrition Values:
Calories 137
Carbohydrate (gm.) 34
Protein (gm.) . . . . n/a
Fat (gm.) 0
% calories from fat 0
Cholesterol (mg.) 0
Sodium (mg.) . . . . n/a

Exchanges:
2 Fruits

Moderate Choice
(Moderate in calories, low in fat, cholesterol)
Gourmet yogurt (medium, 6 oz.)
topped with walnuts (request a
small amount)

Nutrition Values:
Calories 270
Carbohydrate (gm.) 36
Protein (gm.) 8
Fat (gm.) 12
% calories from fat 40
Cholesterol (mg.) 11
Sodium (mg.) . . . . n/a

Exchanges:
1 1/2 Fruits, 1 Milk (2%), 1 Fat

CARVEL ICE CREAM BAKERY

Best Bets

	Calories	Carbohydrate (gm.)	Protein (gm.)	Fat (gm.)	Cholesterol (mg.)	Sodium (mg.)
Carvella	164	16	4	8	61	92
Thinny-Thin	92	16	4	0	4	80
Carvel frozen yogurt (sugar free [contains NutraSweet®] and low fat)	104	20	4	<4	8	80
Lo-Yo	124	20	4	4	16	76
Cone, plain (1)	25	5	1	0	n/a	25
Cone, sugar (1)	45	10	<1	<1	n/a	30

CARVEL ICE CREAM BAKERY (cont.)

Light Choice
(Low in calories, fat, and cholesterol)
Frozen yogurt (small) in plain cone

Nutrition Values:

Calories	129
Carbohydrate (gm.)	25
Protein (gm.)	5
Fat (gm.)	4
% calories from fat	28
Cholesterol (mg.)	8
Sodium (mg.)	105

Exchanges:
1 Starch/Bread, 1/2 Fruit, 1 Fat

Moderate Choice
(Moderate in calories, low in fat, cholesterol)
Carvella (small) in sugar cone

Nutrition Values:

Calories	209
Carbohydrate (gm.)	26
Protein (gm.)	5
Fat (gm.)	9
% calories from fat	30
Cholesterol (mg.)	61
Sodium (mg.)	122

Exchanges:
1 Starch/Bread, 1/2 Fruit, 2 Fats

DAIRY QUEEN

Best Bets

	Calories	Carbohydrate (gm.)	Protein (gm.)	Fat (gm.)	Cholesterol (mg.)	Sodium (mg.)
Vanilla cone (small)	140	22	4	4	15	60
Vanilla cone (regular)	230	36	6	7	20	95
Chocolate cone (regular)	230	36	6	7	20	115
DQ® sandwich	140	24	3	4	5	135
Regular Mr. Misty®	250	63	0	0	0	0
Yogurt cone (regular)	180	38	6	<1	<5	80
Yogurt cone (large)	260	56	9	<1	5	115
Yogurt cup (regular)	170	35	6	<1	<5	70
Yogurt cup (large)	230	49	8	<1	<5	100
Yogurt strawberry sundae (regular)	200	43	6	<1	<5	80

DUTTING IT ALL TOGETHER

Light Choice
(Low in calories, fat, and cholesterol)
DQ® sandwich

Nutrition Values:
Calories 140
Carbohydrate (gm.) 24
Protein (gm.) 3
Fat (gm.) 4
% calories from fat 26
Cholesterol (mg.) 5
Sodium (mg.) 135

Exchanges:
1 Starch/Bread, 1/2 Fruit, 1 Fat

Moderate Choice
(Moderate in calories, low in fat, cholesterol)
Yogurt strawberry sundae (regular)

Nutrition Values:
Calories 200
Carbohydrate (gm.) 43
Protein (gm.) 6
Fat (gm.) . . . . <1
% calories from fat 0
Cholesterol (mg.) . . . . <5
Sodium (mg.) 80

Exchanges:
1 Starch/Bread, 1 Fruit

EVERYTHING YOGURT & SALAD CAFE

Best Bets

	Calories	Carbohydrate (gm.)	Protein (gm.)	Fat (gm.)	Cholesterol (mg.)	Sodium (mg.)
Low-fat frozen yogurt	95	18	3	1	5	30
Nonfat frozen yogurt	80	17	3	0	0	40

DUTTING IT ALL TOGETHER

Light Choice
(Low in calories, fat, and cholesterol)
Frozen yogurt—nonfat (small)
 topped with raisins

Nutrition Values:
Calories 201
Carbohydrate (gm.) 48
Protein (gm.) 6
Fat (gm.) 0
% calories from fat 0
Cholesterol (mg.) 0
Sodium (mg.) 63

Exchanges:
2 Starch/Breads, 1 Fruit

Moderate Choice
(Moderate in calories, low in fat, cholesterol)
Frozen yogurt—low-fat (small)
 topped with granola

Nutrition Values:
Calories 253
Carbohydrate (gm.) 39
Protein (gm.) 8
Fat (gm.) 8
% calories from fat 28
Cholesterol (mg.) 8
Sodium (mg.) 47

Exchanges:
2 Fruits, 1 Milk (2%), 1 Fat

FRESHENS YOGURT

Best Bets

	Calories	Carbohydrate (gm.)	Protein (gm.)	Fat (gm.)	Cholesterol (mg.)	Sodium (mg.)
Low-fat frozen yogurt	96-132*	24	4	3	<20	80
Nonfat frozen yogurt	92-124*	24	4	0	0	72
Sugar- free	68-80*	14	4	0	0	72

Suggested serving sizes: small (6.25 fluid oz.), regular (8.5 fluid oz.)
*Differs slightly according to flavors.

PUTTING IT ALL TOGETHER

Light Choice
(Low in calories, fat, and cholesterol)
Frozen yogurt—nonfat (small)
   topped with fresh strawberries

Nutrition Values:
Calories 230
Carbohydrate (gm.) 55
Protein (gm.) 6
Fat (gm.) 0
% calories from fat 0
Cholesterol (mg.) 0
Sodium (mg.) 115

Exchanges:, 2 Starch/Breads,
1 1/2 Fruits

Moderate Choice
(Moderate in calories, low in fat, cholesterol)
Frozen yogurt—low-fat (regular)
   topped with crushed
   Oreos® (request light)

Nutrition Values:
Calories 342
Carbohydrate (gm.) 65
Protein (gm.) 10
Fat (gm.) 11
% calories from fat 29
Cholesterol (mg.) 43
Sodium (mg.) 296

Exchanges: 1 Starch/Bread, 2 Fruits,
1 Milk (2%), 1 Fat

FUN FOOD FACTS

• Ice cream was a dessert phenomenon from the time of its creation, four thousand years ago, in China. At that point, the milking of farm animals had recently begun and milk was a prized commodity. A favorite dish of the nobility consisted of a soft paste made from overcooked rice, spices, and milk, and packed in snow to solidify. The milk ice was considered a symbol of great wealth. *Extraordinary Origins of Everyday Things, 1987.*

HAAGEN-DAZS

Best Bets

	Calories	Carbohydrate (gm.)	Protein (gm.)	Fat (gm.)	Cholesterol (mg.)	Sodium (mg.)
Sorbet and Cream						
Orange	200	30	3	8	60	30
Raspberry	180	26	3	7	60	30
Frozen Yogurt						
Peach	170	26	6	4	40	45
Vanilla almond crunch	200	29	8	6	50	65
Yogurt Bar						
Raspberry (1)	100	19	3	1	15	20
Sorbet						
Lemon	140	35	0	0	0	20
Raspberry	110	27	0	0	0	15
Nonfat Yogurt						
Vanilla	110	22	5	0	5	75
Coffee	120	25	5	0	5	75

PUTTING IT ALL TOGETHER

Light Choice
(Low in calories, fat, and cholesterol)
Yogurt bar

Nutrition Values:
Calories 100
Carbohydrate (gm.) 19
Protein (gm.) 3
Fat (gm.) 1
% calories from fat 9
Cholesterol (mg.) 15
Sodium (mg.) 20

Exchanges:
1 Starch/Bread

Moderate Choice
(Moderate in calories, low in fat, cholesterol)
Frozen yogurt—vanilla almond crunch
    in sugar cone with chocolate sprinkles

Nutrition Values:
Calories 332
Carbohydrate (gm.) 49
Protein (gm.) 10
Fat (gm.) 11
% calories from fat 30
Cholesterol (mg.) 52
Sodium (mg.) 123

Exchanges:
1 Starch/Bread, 1 1/2 Fruits,
1 Milk (2%), 1 Fat

I CAN'T BELIEVE IT'S YOGURT

Best Bets

	Calories	Carbohydrate (gm.)	Protein (gm.)	Fat (gm.)	Cholesterol (mg.)	Sodium (mg.)
Frozen Yogurt						
Original	108	20	4	3	8	68
Nonfat	80	20	4	0	0	40
Sugar- free Yoglace® (contains NutraSweet®)	80	16	4	0	0	40
Hand Scooped™ Frozen Yogurt						
Classic vanilla	180	30	6	5	25	n/a
Pralines & cream	210	34	5	7	27	n/a
Macadamia mania	220	33	5	7	19	n/a
Peanut butter cup	240	31	6	10	19	n/a

Additional healthy offerings include fruit parfait, 125-calorie hot fudge sundae, and shakes made with yogurt and choice of toppings.

PUTTING IT ALL TOGETHER

Light Choice
(Low in calories, fat, and cholesterol)
Frozen yogurt—sugar-free (6.75 oz.),
   topped with bananas

Nutrition Values:
Calories 166
Carbohydrate (gm.) 35
Protein (gm.) 7
Fat (gm.) 0
% calories from fat 0
Cholesterol (mg.) 0
Sodium (mg.) 68

Exchanges:
2 Starch/Breads

Moderate Choice
(Moderate in calories, low in fat, cholesterol)
Frozen yogurt—hand scooped
   (Macadamia Mania) in sugar cone

Nutrition Values:
Calories 280
Carbohydrate (gm.) 44
Protein (gm.) 6
Fat (gm.) 8
% calories from fat 26
Cholesterol (mg.) 19
Sodium (mg.) 45

Exchanges:
2 Starch/Breads, 1 Fruit, 1 Fat

SWENSEN'S

Best Bets

	Calories	Carbohydrate (gm.)	Protein (gm.)	Fat (gm.)	Cholesterol (mg.)	Sodium (mg.)
Light Ice Cream						
Vanilla	110	15	3	4	10	50
Caramel turtle fudge	120	18	3	4	10	50
Cookies 'n cream	130	20	3	4	10	60
Frozen Yogurt						
Black forest cake	95	21	3	<1	5	130
Triple chocolate	100	21	4	0	0	65
Coconut pineapple	120	26	4	1	5	65
Gourmet -free—Sugar- free						
Blueberry 'n cream	110	17	3	4	10	90
Chocolate raspberry truffle	130	18	3	5	8	80
Vanilla swiss almond	140	15	4	7	10	100

PUTTING IT ALL TOGETHER

Light Choice
(Low in calories, fat, and cholesterol)
Gourmet -free—sugar- free (small) in sugar cone

Nutrition Values:
Calories 190
Carbohydrate (gm.) 29
Protein (gm.) 4
Fat (gm.) 6
% calories from fat 28
Cholesterol (mg.) 8
Sodium (mg.) 125

Exchanges:
1 Starch/Bread, 1 Fruit, 1 Fat

Moderate Choice
(Moderate in calories, low in fat, cholesterol)
Light ice cream - Caramel Turtle Fudge (medium scoop, 8 oz.) served in dish

Nutrition Values:
Calories 240
Carbohydrate (gm.) 36
Protein (gm.) 6
Fat (gm.) 8
% calories from fat 30
Cholesterol (mg.) 20
Sodium (mg) 100

Exchanges:
2 Starch/Breads, 2 Fats

T(BY [THE (OUNTRY'S BEST YOGURT]

Best Bets

Frozen Yogurt

	Calories	Carbohydrate (gm.)	Protein (gm.)	Fat (gm.)	Cholesterol (mg.)	Sodium (mg.)
Regular	130	23	4	3	10	60
Nonfat	110	23	4	<1	<5	45
Sugar free (contains NutraSweet®)	80	18	4	<1	<5	45

Suggested serving sizes: kiddie—3.2 fluid oz., small—5.9 fluid oz., regular—8.2 fluid oz. (Additional healthy offerings include lite bite parfait, lite bite fruit smoothies, "TCBY" Shivers®.)

PUTTING IT ALL TOGETHER

Light Choice
(Low in calories, fat, and cholesterol)
Shiver—frozen yogurt shake (10 oz.)
    with sugar-free yogurt
    and raspberries

Nutrition Values:
Calories 190
Carbohydrate (gm.) 42
Protein (gm.) 9
Fat (gm.) 0
% calories from fat 0
Cholesterol (mg.) 0
Sodium (mg.) 80

Exchanges:
2 Fruits, 1 Milk (2%)

Moderate Choice
(Moderate in calories, low in fat, cholesterol)
Frozen yogurt—nonfat (small, 5.9 oz.)
    topped with almonds (request light)

Nutrition Values:
Calories 247
Carbohydrate (gm.) 37
Protein (gm.) 9
Fat (gm.) 9
% calories from fat 33
Cholesterol (mg.) 7
Sodium (mg.) 68

Exchanges:
1 1/2 Fruits, 1 Milk (2%), 1 Fat

DINNER HOUSES

America is the world's melting pot, and dinner houses show off the cross-cultural influences of American's eating style. American favorites frequently sighted are burgers, barbecued ribs, and prime ribs. Mexican specialties are taco salads, fajitas, and quesadillas. Italy shows off with pizza, lasagna, and pasta primavera. Don't forget the French—quiche and onion soup. Stir-fried dishes and pot stickers from China are slowly appearing. Southwestern cuisine, spread coast to coast by chef Paul Prudhomme, with it's blackened cooking technique and cajun spices was incorporated quickly.

Unfortunately, these chains don't make the road to healthy eating easy. They love to fry, and it shows—from the all too common appetizers of crusty mozzarella sticks, from potato skins to fried shrimp and chicken fingers. Many foods get a healthy start—vegetables, potatoes and pastas. But before they reach your palate they're drenched with cheese or dipped in fats.

But don't get discouraged. Your health-craving taste buds can be satisfied in most of these establishments. Several chains have introduced a few healthier items and provide nutrient facts on the menu. Healthier preparation methods such as stir-frying, grilling, and blackening are used.

Use the advantages of upscale service. Don't be shy about special requests. Apply menu creativity and split, share, or work from the appetizers, salads, and sides. Walk out with tomorrow's lunch or dinner in hand to reach your personal nutrition goals.

Nutrition Pros

■ Newer style cuisines—Asian, Southwestern, Thai—result in tasty, lower fat options.
■ Being upscale and service focused, there's greater willingness to entertain special requests.
■ Multigrain breads and muffins are slowly creeping onto the menu.
■ Dinner salads and baked potatoes are on virtually all menus. Try substituting one for French fries, cole slaw, onion rings, or other fat-laden foods.

Nutrition Cons

■ Portions are too large, even the healthier entrees.
■ Salads can be an illusion. They're generally topped with multiple high-fat nibbles—cheese, avocado, bacon bits.
■ Cheese seems to find its way onto 90% of menu items.
■ Pasta starts off healthy and then often its smothered with cheese or cream sauce.

APPLEBEE'S

Best Bets

Munchies
Munchie sampler (hold cheese sticks)
Parmesan pizza sticks
Burgers
Basic burger
Mushroom burger
Sandwiches
Bacon Cheese Chicken Grill*
(order without bacon and cheese)
Gyro sandwich (request sour
cream sauce on side)
Hickory chicken sandwich
(hold cheese)
Just Right Bites
Chix Stix and Pita*
Chicken pesto primavera
Neighborhood Specialties
Steak or chicken fajitas**
(hold guacamole and sour cream)

Signature items.

Lemon chicken grill
Smothered chicken (hold cheese)
Broiled cajun trout
(Order with choices of fresh steamed
vegetables and new potatoes)
Super Salads
House salad (hold cheese and bacon)
Blackened chicken salad*
(hold cheese, order low-calorie
dressing on side or extra salsa,
request pita bread or bran
muffin rather than garlic bread)
Steak or chicken fajita salad (served
without shell, request pita bread
or bran muffin instead, hold
sour cream, light on cheese, and
extra pico de gallo)
Sides
Salad with meal
Bowl of chili
Combos
Salad and steamed vegetable plate

*Cholesterol-free shortening is used for all
frying.*

PUTTING IT ALL TOGETHER

Light Choice
(Low in calories, fat, and cholesterol)
Salad and steamed vegetable plate
(Hold cheese, bacon; request
low-calorie Italian dressing on side)
Milk - 2% (8 oz.)

Nutrition Values:

Calories 400
Carbohydrate (gm.) 55
Protein (gm.) 18
Fat (gm.) 14
% calories from fat 31
Cholesterol (mg.) 84
Sodium (mg.) 903

Exchanges: 1 1/2 Starch/Breads,
4 Vegetables, 1 Milk , 3 Fats

Moderate Choice:
(Moderate in calories, low in fat and cholesterol)
Munchie sampler (Hold cheese sticks
and split with someone)
Gyro sandwich (Request sauce on
the side.)

Nutrition Values:

Calories 735
Carbohydrate (gm.) 75
Protein (gm.) 42
Fat (gm.) 30
% calories from fat 37
Cholesterol (mg.) 115
Sodium (mg.) 1778

Exchanges: 3 Starch/Breads, 4 Meats
(medium), 3 Vegetables, 1 Fat

BENNIGAN'S

Best Bets

Great Beginnings
Peel & eat shrimp
Veggie trio (request not fried
    and served with reduced-calorie
    salad dressing)

Lite
Grilled shrimp
Steamed vegetable platter
Citrus chicken
Tropical grilled chicken salad
Turkey burger

Chilled Salads
Bennigan's house salad (hold avocado,
    bacon)
Deli salad (hold cheese, request
    fresh-baked bread)
Fajita salad (serve without shell,
    hold guacamole and sour cream,
    bring extra salsa)
Chicken salad
Spinach salad (hold bacon)

Warm Salads
Oriental chicken salad
Charleston chicken salad (hold cheese,
    serve with fresh-baked bread,
    low-calorie dressing or salsa
    on side)
Mesa chicken salad (hold avocado,
    serve with fresh-baked bread,
    low-calorie dressing or salsa on
    side)
Chicken taco salad (order without shell,
    hold guacamole, sour cream,
    served with fresh-baked bread,
    salsa on side)

Classic Sandwiches
French dip (hold cheese)
Chicken Philly (hold cheese)

Chicken Sandwiches
Create your own—choose from
    sauteed mushrooms or onions, BBQ
    sauce, marinara sauce, cajun or
    Mesquite seasoning

Burger Platters
Name your own burger—choose from
    sauteed mushrooms, onions,
    jalapenos, BBQ sauce (Request
    baked potato or dinner salad
    instead of French fries)

Chicken
Chicken teriyaki (2 breasts) (order
    vegetable medley or salad and
    doggie bag (take 1/2 chicken home)

Seafood
Grilled shrimp
Lobster and shrimp marinara
    (served with fresh-baked bread)
Spicy shrimp primavera

Sides
Baked potato
Dinner salad

*Bennigan's uses 100% cholesterol-free veg-
etable cooking oil and offers low-calorie Italian salad dressing. Grey Poupon® Dijon
Mustard is available as noted on menu.*

BENNIGAN'S (cont.)

PUTTING IT ALL TOGETHER

Light Choice
(Low in calories, fat, and cholesterol)

Peel and eat shrimp with cocktail sauce (appetizer)

Bennigan's House salad (Hold avocado and bacon and request low-calorie Italian [2 tbsp.] on the side)

Fresh-baked bread (2 slices) with butter (1 pat)

White wine - 1 glass (6 oz.)†

Nutrition Values:
Calories 676
Carbohydrate (gm.) 60
Protein (gm.) 46
Fat (gm.) 14
% calories from fat 19
Cholesterol (mg.) 329*
Sodium (mg.) 1864
Cholesterol high because of shrimp.
Exchanges: 3 Starch/Breads, 3 Meats (lean), 3 Vegetables

†Alcohol not accounted for in exchanges.

Moderate Choice
(Moderate in calories, low in fat and cholesterol)

Name your own burger—lite burger with sauteed mushrooms and BBQ sauce

Baked potato (instead of French fries, Request Dijon mustard on the side)

Deep dish apple cobbler a la mode (share)

Nutrition Values:
Calories 988
Carbohydrate (gm.) 115
Protein (gm.) 42
Fat (gm.) 40
% calories from fat 36
Cholesterol (mg. 133
Sodium (mg.) 1424

Exchanges: 6 Starch/Breads
3 Meats (medium), 1 Vegetable, 1 Fruit
4 Fats

FUN FOOD FACTS

• Caesar salad, consisting of greens tossed with garlic vinaigrette dressing, grated Parmesan cheese, croutons, egg, and anchovies, is said to have been created in 1924 by Italian chef Caesar Cardini, who owned a restaurant in Tijuana, Mexico. *Food Lover's Companion, 1990.*

• The longest kebab ever was 2,066 feet, 11 inches long, made by the Namibian Children's Home at Windhoek, Namibia, on September 21, 1991. *Guinness Book of Records, 1993.*

BLACK-EYED PEA

Best Bets

Appetizers
Big bowl of red beans and rice (served
with cornbread)

Soups and salads
Dinner salad (hold cheese)
Soup and salad (if brothy soup)
Charbroiled chicken salad (hold
cheese)
Grilled tuna steak salad (hold cheese)

Sandwiches
Charbroiled chicken breast sandwich
Grilled tuna steak sandwich

Entrees (Split or request doggie bag.
Entrees include 2 side dishes, roll,
or cornbread.)
Charbroiled pork chops (2)
Charbroiled chicken breast

Baked whitefish
Grilled tuna steak (8-oz.
uncooked weight)
Vegetable plate (5 vegetables served
with whole-wheat roll or cornbread)
Stuffed Baked Potatoes (with salad)
Cheese broccoli (light on cheese sauce)
Mom's meatloaf
Juicy pot roast

Sides
Black-eyed peas
Green beans
Glazed carrots
Red beans and rice
Kernel corn
Mashed potatoes (hold the gravy)
Rice

Low-calorie Italian dressing and low-fat milk are available.

PUTTING IT ALL TOGETHER

Light Choice
(Low in calories, fat, and cholesterol)
Grilled tuna steak sandwich (request
sauce on side)
Glazed carrots (side item)
Black-eyed peas (side item)

Nutrition Values:
Calories 613
Carbohydrate (gm.) 71
Protein (gm.) 41
Fat (gm.) 23
% calories from fat 34
Cholesterol (mg.) 77
Sodium (mg.) 1053

Exchanges: 4 Starch/Breads, 4 Meats
(lean), 2 Vegetables, 1 Fat

Moderate Choice
(Moderate in calories, low in fat and cholesterol)
Juicy pot roast potato (light on gravy)
Dinner salad (Hold cheese and request
Thousand Island [2 tbsp.] and
lemon wedges on side.)
Milk (2%) - 8 oz.

Nutrition Values:
Calories 721
Carbohydrate (gm.) 76
Protein (gm.) 46
Fat (gm.) 27
% calories from fat 34
Cholesterol (mg.) 114
Sodium (mg.) 1124

Exchanges: 3 Starch/Breads, 3 Meats
(medium), 2 Vegetables, 1 Milk, 2 Fats

CHILI'S

Best Bets

Starters
Soup of the day — cup or bowl
(if brothy)
Chili (hold cheese)

Salads
Caribbean (hold tortilla strips, request
low-cal dressing on side)
Grilled tuna (request low-cal dressing
on side)
Chicken Frisco™ (request low-cal
dressing on side)
Southwest Salad (hold guacamole)
Dinner salad (request low-calorie
dressing on side)

Southwest Grill
Fajitas, chicken (share single order)
Grilled chicken
Open Range
Tuna steak sandwich
Veggie tacos
Chicken tacos (hold sour cream)
Chili's special soft tacos
Sides
Fresh steamed vegetables
Homemade mashed potatoes
Sweet corn cobbette (request
no buttersauce)
Dessert
Nonfat frozen yogurt

No-fat vinaigrette and low-calorie ranch dressing are available. Substitution available upon request. Chili's uses cholesterol-free 100% vegetable oil.

PUTTING IT ALL TOGETHER

Light Choice
(Low in calories, fat, and cholesterol)
Fajita's (Charbroiled chicken.
Request 6 tortillas and share.)
Dinner salad (Request low-calorie
ranch [2 tbsp.] and lemon wedges on
the side)
Nonfat frozen yogurt (share)

Nutrition Values:
Calorie	713
Carbohydrate (gm.)	86
Protein (gm.)	35
Fat (gm.)	28
% calories from fat	35
Cholesterol (mg.)	78
Sodium (mg.)	944

Exchanges:
3 Starch/Breads, 3 Meats (lean)
3 Vegetables, 1 Fruit , 4 Fats

Moderate Choice
(Moderate in calories, low in fat and cholesterol)
Chicken Frisco™ (hold avocado,
light on almonds)
Sourdough bun (request on side)

Nutrition Values:
Calories	813
Carbohydrate (gm.)	84
Protein (gm.)	53
Fat (gm.)	33
% calories from fat	36
Cholesterol (mg.)	256*
Sodium (mg.)	1433

*High in cholesterol due to egg in salad.

Exchanges:
4 Starch/Breads, 5 Meats (medium)
3 Vegetables, 1 Fat

FUDDRUCKERS

Best Bets

Grilled chicken breast sandwich
Original (skinless breast)
BBQ (skinless breast)

Grilled fish sandwiches
New Orleans fish sandwich with spicy cajun sauce

Fuddruckers has a unique concept. You order a basic sandwich and then top it with fresh vegetables and condiments. Take advantage of this by loading on low-calorie veggies and toppings.

Salads & Soup
Grilled country chicken salad (request garlic ranch dressing on side)
Grilled chicken taco salad with Tex-Mex fixins
Beef taco salad with Tex-Mex fixins
Dinner side salad
Soup (if brothy)

Hamburgers
The original (4 oz. uncooked weight; add mushrooms and grilled onions.)

PUTTING IT ALL TOGETHER

Light Choice
(Low in calories, fat, and cholesterol)

The Original Hamburger (4 oz. uncooked weight) on hamburger roll. Top with lettuce, tomato, ketchup, and relish
Dinner salad with vinegar

Nutrition Values:
Calories 625
Carbohydrate (gm.) 58
Protein (gm.) 36
Fat (gm.) 29
% calories from fat 42
Cholesterol (mg.) 99
Sodium (mg.) 1437

Exchanges:
3 Starch/Breads. 3 Meats (medium), 2 Vegetables, 2 Fat

Moderate Choice
(Moderate in calories, low in fat , cholesterol)

BBQ chicken sandwich (grilled breast) on roll (top with lettuce, tomato, and raw onions)
Fudd fries (split order)

Nutrition Values:
Calories 633
Carbohydrate (gm.) 67
Protein (gm.) .45
Fat (gm.) 20
% calories from fat 28
Cholesterol (mg.) 109
Sodium (mg.) 1905

Exchanges:
4 Starch/Breads, 4 Meats (medium), 1 Vegetable, 2 Fats

GROUND ROUND

Best Bets

Appetizers
Peel and eat shrimp (12)
Mexican pizza (order as entree)
Salads (request low-cal dressing on side)
House salad
Taco salad (serve without shell, hold cheese and sour cream, request extra salsa)
Charbroiled chicken breast salad
Great Lunch Breaks
Vegetable stir fry
Deli sandwich—ham, turkey or roast beef (Request substitute house salad for French fries and cole slaw)
Baked potato and house salad (hold sour cream)
Seafood
Baked Boston scrod

Charbroiled swordfish (10 oz. uncooked weight) (share)
Shrimp fajita (hold sour cream, request extra pico de gallo)
Shrimp stir fry (choose salad as side)
International Favorites
Chicken or steak fajitas (hold cheese, request extra pico de gallo)
Steak
6-oz. top sirloin steak (uncooked weight)
Chicken
All American chicken grille (New Orleans or Santa Fe preparation)
Chicken stir fry (choose rice and salad as sides)
Burgers
Mushroom burger
Sandwiches
French dip (substitute house salad for French fries)
Virginian (hold cheese, substitute house salad for onion rings)

PUTTING IT ALL TOGETHER

Light Choice
(Low in calories, fat, and cholesterol)
Shrimp stir fry served with rice
House salad with oil (2 tsp. olive oil) and vinegar (2 tbsp.)

Nutrition Values:
Calories 611
Carbohydrate (gm.) 72
Protein (gm.) 33
Fat (gm.) 21
% calories from fat 31
Cholesterol (mg.) 175*
Sodium (mg.) 974
*Shrimp is high in cholesterol.

Exchanges: 3 1/2 Starch/Breads, 3 Meats (lean) , 3 Vegetables, 2 Fats

Moderate Choice
(Moderate in calories, low in fat and cholesterol)
Charbroiled swordfish (take half home)
Baked potato with 2 tbsp. sour cream
Vegetable (hold butter)
House salad with French dressing (2 tbsp.) on side

Nutrition Values:
Calories 677
Carbohydrate (gm.) 70
Protein (gm.) 44
Fat (gm.) 27
% calories from fat 36
Cholesterol (mg.) 21
Sodium (mg.) 1138

Exchanges: 3 Starch/Breads, 4 Meats (lean), 3 Vegetables, 3 Fats

HARD ROCK CAFE

Best Buys

Starters
Mom's chicken noodle soup
Hard Rock & Roll Chili
Salads
Cafe Chef Salad (hold cheese, have dressing on side)
"The Kingdom" Chicken Salad (hold hot bacon dressing, request dressing on side)
"South of the Border" salad (hold tortilla shell, cheese, and sour cream)
Sandwiches
California club (hold cheese and mayonnaise)

HRC's Daily Specials
Catch of the day (baked, broiled, grilled)
HRC's grilled orange chicken with baked potato and ranch beans
HRC's famous grilled fajitas (chicken, beef, vegetables or shrimp, hold guacamole and sour cream)
"Pig sandwich" with baked potato and ranch beans
Hot Platters
HRC's country char-broiled burger with ranch beans (hold fries)
Vegetable burger (hold fries and substitute ranch beans)
Desserts
Etta B's Homemade Apple Pie (hold toppings)
Key lime pie (hold whipped cream)
Homemade strawberry short cake (hold whipped cream)

PUTTING IT ALL TOGETHER

Light Choice
(Low in calories, fat, and cholesterol)

HRC's famous grilled fajitas—grilled shrimp (3 tortillas, hold guacamole and sour cream)

Nutrition Values:
Calories 567
Carbohydrate (gm.) 70
Protein (gm.) 33
Fat (gm.) 19
% calories from fat 31
Cholesterol (mg.) 175*
Sodium (mg.) 1150
Shrimp is high in cholesterol.

Exchanges: 3 Starch/Breads, 3 Meats (lean) , 2 Vegetables, 2 Fats

Moderate Choice
(Moderate in calories, low in fat and cholesterol)

HRC's country char-broiled burger (hold French fries)
Salad with 2 tbsp. ranch dressing
Homemade strawberry short cake (hold whipped cream and share)

Nutrition Values:
Calories 782
Carbohydrate (gm.) 73
Protein (gm.) .39
Fat (gm.) 38
% calories from fat 44
Cholesterol (mg.) 95
Sodium (mg.) 1180

Exchanges: 3 Starch/Breads, 4 Meats (medium), 2 Vegetables, 1 Fruit 3 Fats

HOULIHAN'S

Best Bets

Pastas and Pizzas
Chicken and garden vegetable linguini
Shrimp linguini
Specialties
Mesa salmon grille
Today's fresh fish (broiled)
Blackened chicken quesadilla
  (hold cheese)
Chicken stir-fry
Vegetable stir-fry
Sizzling fajitas (hold guacamole,
  cheese, sour cream; request extra salsa)
Sandwiches and Burgers
Blackened cajun burger (hold cheese)
Blackened chicken grille (hold cheese)
Teriyaki chicken grille (hold cheese)

Salads
Garden salad (hold croutons)
Chinese chicken salad (hold peanuts,
  light on noodles, request dressing
  on side)
Cashew chicken salad (hold avocado
  and request light on cashews)
Chicken Monterey (serve without shell,
  hold guacamole dressing and
  request extra salsa)
Combos
Loaded baked potato (request top with
  black bean chili; order with garden
  salad)
Hot stacked beef and cheese (hold
  cheese; order with garden salad)
Black bean chili (order with garden
  salad)
Dessert
Fruit sorbet

PUTTING IT ALL TOGETHER

Light Choice
Low in calories, fat, and cholesterol

Cashew chicken salad (light on
  cashews, hold avocado) with Lemon
  Dijon dressing on side
Roll or crackers

Nutrition Values:
Calories 518
Carbohydrate (gm.) 35
Protein (gm.) .45
Fat (gm.) 24
% calories from fat 42
Cholesterol (mg.) 96
Sodium (mg.) 1189

Exchanges: 1 Starch/Bread, 5 Meats
(lean), 3 Vegetables, 2 Fats

Moderate Choice
(Moderate in calories, low in fat and cholesterol)

Chicken and garden vegetable linguini
Garden salad with French dressing
  on side (2 tbsp.) with vinegar, hold
  croutons
Fruit sorbet (share)

Nutrition Values:
Calories 809
Carbohydrate (gm.) 84
Protein (gm.) .48
Fat (gm.) 33
% calories from fat 37
Cholesterol (mg.) 158
Sodium (mg.) 1499

Exchanges: 4 Starch/Breads, 4 Meats
(lean), 2 Vegetables, 1 Fruit, 4 Fats

HOUSTON'S

Best Bets

Burgers and the club
Hickory burger
Salads
House salad (hold croutons and
  bacon) with dressing, lemon wedges,
  or vinegar on side
Grilled chicken salad with dressing
  on side
Pizza (not available in some locations)
Margherita
Thai chicken

Fresh Fish (with couscous and house
  salad)
Chicken, Beef, and Ribs
Roasted chicken (order with couscous;
  share or ask for doggie bag)
Barbecue chicken (substitute couscous
  and house salad for beans, fries, and
  cole slaw)
This and That (sides)
Couscous (large serving)
Dessert
Seasonal fresh fruit (when available)

Some items are fried in 100% vegetable oil

PUTTING IT ALL TOGETHER

Light Choice:
Low in calories, fat, and cholesterol
Barbecue chicken breast
  (request doggie bag or share)
Iron skillet beans
Couscous
House salad (hold bacon) with
  olive oil (2 tsp.) and vinegar on side
Seasonal fresh fruit (share)

Nutrition Values:
Calories 721
Carbohydrate (gm.) 84
Protein (gm.) .46
Fat (gm.) 24
% calories from fat 30
Cholesterol (mg.) 186
Sodium (mg.) 1635

Exchanges: 4 Starch/Breads, 4 Meats
(lean) , 2 Vegetables, 1 Fruit, 2 Fats

Moderate Choice
(Moderate calories, low fat and cholesterol)
House salad with honey mustard
  dressing (2 tbsp.) on side (hold
  bacon)
Margherita pizza (share)
Wine—white (6 oz.)*

Nutrition Values:
Calories 883
Carbohydrate (gm.) 93
Protein (gm.) 23
Fat (gm.) 35
% calories from fat 35
Cholesterol (mg.) 143
Sodium (mg.) 1714

Exchanges: 4 Starch/Breads, 1 Meat
(medium), 3 Vegetables, 5 Fats
  *Alcohol not accounted for in exchanges

RUBY TUESDAY'S

Best Bets

Salad Bar, Soups & Combinations
Ruby's salad bar extravaganza
(choose with care)
Salad and Broccoli Jack n' Cheddar
baked potato (hold butter
and Parmesan)

Sandwiches & Burgers (request
multigrain bun; substitute baked
potato or trip to salad bar)
Cajun chicken (hold remoulade sauce)
All-American burger
Smokey mountain burger

Entree salads
Chicken fajita salad (hold cheese and
ranch dressing; request extra salsa)

Specialties (substitute baked potato
for fries)
Smokey mountain chicken
(hold cheese)
Cajun chicken (hold remoulade sauce)
Grilled or blackened fish (hold garlic
cheese bread)

Open-faced chicken breast sandwich
(hold cheese)
Fit n' trim fish or chicken with dressing
on side
Steamed vegetable plate (4 vegetables
with baked potato)

Fabulous Fajitas and More
Classic steak or chicken fajita (hold
sour cream and guacamole)
Classic shrimp fajita (hold sour cream
and guacamole)

Ruby's Signature Entrees (split
entree and order extra trip to
salad bar)
Top sirloin (10 oz. uncooked
weight; hold butter)
Blackened or grilled fish (12-oz.
uncooked weight)

Sides
Steamed vegetables
Seasoned rice or baked potato

FUN FOOD FACTS

• Cajun cooking comes from descendants of French Acadians whom the
British forced from their Nova Scotian homeland to Louisiana in 1785.
The name Acadian Cagian eventually became Cajun. Cajun cooking is
a combination of French and Southern cuisines made famous by chef
Paul Prudhomme. *Food Lover's Companion, 1990.*

PUTTING IT ALL TOGETHER

Light Choice:
(Low in calories, fat, and cholesterol)
Salad and Broccoli Jack n' Cheddar
   baked potato (hold butter and
   Parmesan; light on Jack cheese)
Salad bar with olive oil (2 tsp.) and
   vinegar dressing (See page 6 for
   salad bar information.)

Nutrition Values:
Calories 573
Carbohydrate (gm.) 86
Protein (gm.) 21
Fat (gm.) 20
% calories from fat 31
Cholesterol (mg.) 23
Sodium (mg.) 832

Exchanges:
4 Starch/Breads, 1 Meat (medium),
4 Vegetables, 2 Fats

Moderate Choice
(Moderate in calories, low in fat and cholesterol)
Top sirloin (10 oz. uncooked weight
   shared)
Seasoned rice (shared)
Whole wheat bread sticks (2)
Salad bar with Blue cheese dressing
   (2 tbsp.) and vinegar (See page 6
   for salad bar information.)
Wine—white (6 oz.)*

Nutrition Values:
Calories 930
Carbohydrate (gm.) 73
Protein (gm.) 45
Fat (gm.) 40
% calories from fat 39
Cholesterol (mg.) 107
Sodium (mg.) 1506

Exchanges:
4 Starch/Breads, 4 Meats (medium),
3 Vegetables, 4 Fats
   Alcohol not accounted for in exchanges.

T.G.I. FRIDAY'S

Best Bets

Appetizers
Thai chicken
Pot stickers
Peel and eat shrimp

Soup and combinations
Fresh vegetable medley

Salads and lighter fare
Friday's house salad (hold garlic bread)
Friday's house salad with shrimp (hold garlic bread)
Spinach salad (hold bacon and garlic bread)
Charbroiled fajita salad without shell (hold cheese, serve with extra salsa)
Friday's Thai chicken salad with dressing on side
Chinese chicken salad with dressing on side

Friday's Lite
Fresh vegetable baguette
Friday's garden burger
Pacific coast tuna sandwich
Pacific coast chicken sandwich
Salad and baked potato

Sandwiches
California chargrilled turkey
Charbroiled chicken (hold mayonnaise)
Blackened-Cajun chicken (hold cheese and mayonnaise)
French dip (hold cheese)
Fajita steak baguette (hold cheese)

Hamburger (6 oz.)
Name your own burger (choose from bell peppers, black beans, burgundy wine sauce, cajun seasonings, mushrooms, onions, pineapple, salsa)

Southwestern
Beef or chicken fajitas (hold cheese and sour cream)

Pasta & Pizza
Spicy cajun chicken pasta
Linguini with shrimp
Pasta Santa Fe
Bistro pizza
Create your own (choose from bell peppers, black olives, Canadian bacon, ham, mushrooms, onions, pineapple, tomato)

Friday's Classic
Steak on a stick with plain baked potato
Fish of the day (with rice, chef's vegetable selection or house salad)
Herb grilled chicken
Blackened-Cajun chicken

Sides
Chef's vegetable selection
Brown rice pilaf
Black beans and brown rice
Baked potato (unloaded)

Fat-free California French and fat-free Italian herb dressings are available. Nutrition information is provided for lite entrees.

PUTTING IT ALL TOGETHER

Light Choice
(Low in calories, fat, and cholesterol)
Fresh vegetable baguette
Sherbet (share)

Nutrition Values:
Calories	588
Carbohydrate (gm.)	88
Protein (gm.)	11
Fat (gm.)	15
% calories from fat	23
Cholesterol (mg.)	n/a
Sodium (mg.)	n/a

Exchanges:
4 Starch/Breads, 1 Meat (medium) ,
2 Vegetables, 1 Fruit, 2 Fats

Moderate Choice
(Moderate in calories, low in fat and cholesterol)
Name your own burger (6 oz.)
   with bell peppers, mushrooms,
   and cajun spices
Black beans and rice
Beer (light) (12 oz.)*

Nutrition Values:
Calories	725
Carbohydrate (gm.)	70
Protein (gm.)	34
Fat (gm.)	25
% calories from fat	31
Cholesterol (mg.)	77
Sodium (mg.)	1524

Exchanges:
3 Starch/Breads, 4 Meats (medium),
1 Vegetable, 1 Fat
   Alcohol not accounted for in exchanges

FAMILY RESTAURANTS

Open round the clock and always offering a bottomless cup of coffee, sandwiches and fries, meat and potatoes. That's what family restaurants generally are about. Thousands of these establishments line America's highways, especially in the southeast, north and south central regions. They provide table service without tablecloths or white-glove treatment and promise a friendly server who will keep your coffee cup full.

Several family restaurant chains offer special menus for tots and seniors. Unfortunately, kid's menus are short and often filled with high-fat favorites—grilled cheese, hot dogs, and chicken fingers. The seniors' menus (for folks over 55 or 60) offer reduced portions or reduced prices or both. In that case, it might be worthwhile to boast about your age.

How is this restaurant sector responding to customers' demands for healthier eating options? They've made some changes, but most chains still believe customers' talk healthy but order to satisfy taste buds. As one research and development director said, "People still consider eating out a special occasion, even if it happens an average of four times per week."

Unlike fast food chains, family restaurants don't typically provide nutrition or ingredient information. No chains provide it for the entire menu. Several restaurants mark the healthier offerings on their menu or offer a brochure with nutrition information.

Whether you order from the lighter side, from the seniors' menu, or from the regular offerings, a healthy meal is possible but challenging. Pick and choose carefully, and try some creative strategies.

Nutrition Pros

■ No rolls, crackers, cheese, or jellies are on the table.
■ Healthier soups can help you feel satisfied without adding too many calories or fat.
■ Seniors' menus might offer smaller portions.
■ Interesting condiments are available to help spice up your meal—teriyaki sauce, salsa, lemon, vinegars, low-calorie dressings.
■ Frozen yogurt is beginning to show up as a healthier dessert option.

Nutrition Cons

■ Portions are larger than needed, even the healthier choices.
■ Soups often contain lots of fat.
■ Chicken is often battered, fried, smothered with cheese, or topped with gravy.
■ Pasta usually comes in cream sauce or covered with cheese.
■ French fries, onion rings, and creamy coleslaw are standard with many meals.

BAKERS SQUARE

Best Bets for Breakfast

Specialties
Seasonal fruit
Omelettes
Eggstra'Special Omelette
On the Light Side
Continental breakfast (rolls, muffins)
One egg (hold the bacon or sausage)

Side Orders
Cereal
Oatmeal
Muffin
Toast or English muffin
Pancakes, French toast (grilled, not
fried), waffles (with syrup on side)

PUTTING IT ALL TOGETHER

Light Choice
(Low in calories, fat, and cholesterol)
Order a la carte
Egg (poached)
English muffin with 2 tbsp. jelly
and 1 pat margarine
Milk (2%)

Nutrition Values:
Calorie 423
Carbohydrate (gm.) 52
Protein (gm.) 20
Fat (gm.) 15
% calories from fat 31
Cholesterol (mg.) 230*
Sodium (mg.) 721
High in cholesterol
Exchanges: 2 Starch/Breads, 1 Meat
(medium), 1/2 Fruit, 1 Milk, 1 Fat

Moderate Choice
(Moderate in calories, low in fat, cholesterol)
Eggstra'Special Omelette (hold ham)
Whole-wheat toast with jelly (1 pkg.)
Seasonal fruit
Coffee with 2 tbsp. regular milk

Nutrition Values:
Calories 581
Carbohydrate (gm.) 54
Protein (gm.) 42
Fat (gm.) 23
% calories from fat 36
Cholesterol (mg.) 32
Sodium (mg.) 1485

Exchanges: 2 Starch/Breads, 5 Meats
(medium), 1 Vegetable, 1 Fruit

Best Bets for Lunch or Dinner

Soups and Appetizers
Crock or cup of soup (broth based)
Crock or cup of chili
Super Burgers
Hamburger (5 oz. uncooked weight)
with coleslaw or garden salad
The Light Side
Bacon, lettuce, and tomato deluxe
(hold mayo, order side salad)

1/2 tuna sandwich with salad
1/2 turkey sandwich with salad
Soup (broth based), salad, and bread
Chili, salad, and bread
Light choice chicken
On salads, request low-calorie
dressing on the side.

On the Side
Baked potato (plain)
Rice pilaf
Broccoli florets (hold cheese sauce)
Garden salad
Main Meals
Stir-fry chicken
Orange roughy (hold cheese sauce, tartar sauce, and order rice pilaf or baked potato)
Dijon chicken (hold cheese sauce, cheese, and order rice pilaf or baked potato)
Entree Salads
Chicken breast salad with dressing on side
Chef salad without cheese and with dressing on side
Taco salad with extra salsa and without tortilla shell, cheese, or sour cream
Bakers choice salad
Pasta
Chicken marinara

Sandwiches
French dip with coleslaw or garden salad
Turkey sandwich with Dijon mustard on side (hold mayo)
Chicken breast sandwich
Pitas
Chicken fajita pita with extra salsa on side (hold cheese and guacamole)
Stir-fry chicken pita (hold cheese)
Square Deal Lunches
Bayou chicken sandwich (hold French fries)
Smokey mountain BBQ chicken sandwich (hold French Fries)
Square Deal Dinners
Honey mustard chicken with garden salad, dressing on side
Chicken mixed grill with garden salad, dressing on side (hold butter Parmesan sauce)
Stir-fry chicken with garden salad, dressing on side

PUTTING IT ALL TOGETHER

Light Choice for Lunch or Dinner
(Low in calories, fat, and cholesterol)
1/2 Turkey sandwich with mustard, no mayo
Garden salad with lo-cal ranch (2 tbsp.) on side
2% Milk (8 oz.)

Nutrition Values:

Calories	452
Carbohydrate (gm.)	38
Protein (gm.)	40
Fat (gm.)	16
% calories from fat	32
Cholesterol (mg.)	77
Sodium (mg.)	1309

Exchanges: 1 Starch/Breads, 3 Meats (lean), 2 Vegetables, 1 Milk

Moderate Choice for Lunch or Dinner
(Moderate in calories, low in fat, cholesterol)
Chicken marinara (light on cheese)
Special bread (1 slice)
Garden salad with lo-cal ranch (2 tbsp.) on side
Cherry pie, split

Nutrition Values:

Calories	821
Carbohydrate (gm.)	93
Protein (gm.)	47
Fat (gm.)	31
% calories from fat	34
Cholesterol (mg.)	157
Sodium (mg.)	2075*

* High in sodium

Exchanges: 5 Starch/Breads, 4 Meats (medium), 1 Vegetable, 1 Fruit, 2 Fats

BIG BOY RESTAURANT AND BAKE SHOP

Bets Bets for Breakfast

Eggs with toast
French toast, if grilled, not fried
Belgian waffle (available with
  fresh strawberries)

Hotcakes
Mexican omelette (split with
  hotcakes order)

For all choices, hold butter and get syrup on side. EggBeaters™ is available.

PUTTING IT ALL TOGETHER

Light Choice for Breakfast
(Low in calories, fat, and cholesterol)
Eggs (2), made with EggBeaters
Biscuit with jam (1 pkg.)
Grapefruit juice (6 oz.)
Coffee with 2 tbsp. milk

Nutrition Values:
Calories. 306
Carbohydrate (gm.) 48
Protein (gm.) 14
Fat (gm.) 6
% calories from fat 18
Cholesterol (mg.) 4
Sodium (mg.) 359

Exchanges: 2 Starch/Breads, 1 Meat
(lean), 1 1/2 Fruits, 1 Fat

Moderate Choice for Breakfast
(Moderate in calories, low in fat, cholesterol)
Belgian waffle with fresh strawberries
  and 3 tbsp. regular pancake syrup
Coffee with 2 tbsp. regular milk

Nutrition Values:
Calories 579
Carbohydrate (gm.) 99
Protein (gm.) 10
Fat (gm.) 19
% calories from fat 29
Cholesterol (mg.) 6
Sodium (mg.) 979

Exchanges: 4 Starch/Breads, 2 Fruits,
3 Fats

Best Bets for Lunch and Dinner

	Calories	Carbohydrate (gm.)	Protein (gm.)	Fat (gm.)	Cholesterol (mg.)	Sodium (mg.)
Dinners						
Chicken 'n vegetable stir-fry	562	68	43	14	68	750
Vegetable stir-fry	408	74	9	10	0	703
Cajun chicken	349	20	38	13	65	612
Breast of chicken	349	20	38	13	65	342

	Calories	Carbohydrate (gm.)	Protein (gm.)	Fat (gm.)	Cholesterol (mg.)	Sodium (mg.)
Breast of chicken with mozzarella	370	24	42	12	76	353
Baked or broiled cod	364	20	43	12	68	371
Baked or broiled cod Dijon	427	21	44	18	68	567
Cajun cod	364	20	43	12	68	461
Spaghetti marinara	450	87	15	6	8	761

Nutrition information based on salad without dressing, 1 slice oat bran bread, and margarine.

Pitas

Turkey pita (sandwich only)	224	24	22	5	75	833
Breast of chicken with mozzarella (sandwich only)	404	26	42	13	76	421

Soups and Salads

Dinner salad, no dressing	19	4	1	0	0	11
Chicken breast salad with Dijon	391	31	42	11	65	415
Cabbage soup, cup	37	8	2	0	1	623
bowl	43	9	2	1	1	727

Breads and Sides

Roll	139	30	3	0	2	187
Rice	114	25	3	0	0	633
Baked potato	163	37	5	0	0	7
Corn	90	21	3	1	0	1
Green beans	28	6	2	0	0	1
Carrots	35	8	1	0	0	38
Peas	77	13	6	0	0	131
Mixed vegetables	27	5	2	0	0	42
Buttermilk dressing	36	4	0	2	10	151

Dessert

Frozen yogurt	72	16	2	0	0	31
No-no frozen dessert	75	17	2	0	0	36
Frozen yogurt shake	184	36	8	0	2	127

Nutrition information provided on the menu for Heart Smart® menu listings

BIG BOY (cont.)

Best Bets for Lunch or Dinner

Appetizers, soups, and salads
Soup, salad, and fruit bar (choose carefully)
Cabbage soup
Chili, cup or bowl
Vegetables
Super salads and pitas
Tuna salad or pita
Shrimp and crab salad or pita
Shrimp salad
Roasted chicken breast salad
Turkey pita
Health Smart® menu
Chicken 'n' seafood stir-fry
Chicken 'n' vegetable stir-fry
Cajun chicken
Cod Dijon, baked or broiled

Cajun cod
Spaghetti marinara
Chicken breast with mozzarella pita
Vegetable stir-fry
Frozen yogurt or shake
No-no frozen dessert
Sandwiches
Brawny Lad (substitute vegetables or baked potato for onion rings)
Hot turkey sandwich
Broiled chicken sandwich
Dinners
Chicken and vegetable stir-fry
Boneless breast of chicken
Broiled cracker crumb cod
Sides
Dinner roll or bran muffin
Rice or baked potato
Hot vegetables

Health Smart® menu is low in fat, sodium, and cholesterol. Nutrition information for Health Smart items is on the menu.

PUTTING IT ALL TOGETHER

Light Choice for Lunch or Dinner
(Low in calories, fat, and cholesterol)
Vegetable beef soup, cup
Turkey pita with 2 tbsp. low-calorie buttermilk dressing on side
Frozen yogurt shake

Nutrition Values:
Calories 504
Carbohydrate (gm.) 74
Protein (gm.) 33
Fat (gm.) 7
% calories from fat 13
Cholesterol (mg.) 97
Sodium (mg.) 1734

Exchanges: 3 Starch/Breads, 3 Vegetables, 4 Meats (lean), 1 Fruit

Moderate Choice for Lunch or Dinner
(Moderate in calories, low in fat, cholesterol)
Cabbage soup, cup
Cajun cod (from Health Smart menu)
Baked potato with mustard on side
Steamed carrots
Frozen yogurt (3 oz.)

Nutrition Values:
Calories 699
Carbohydrate (gm.) 89
Protein (gm.) 58
Fat (gm.) 14
% calories from fat 18
Cholesterol (mg.) 77
Sodium (mg.) 1178

Exchanges: 4 Starch/Breads, 5 Meats (lean), 2 vegetables, 1 fruit

BOB EVANS FARMS

Best Bets for Breakfast

Omelette Breakfast
Western omelette (substitute
  EggBeaters™)
The Lighter Side
Oatmeal breakfast
Eggbeaters® breakfast
A La Carte
One fresh egg (regular or
  substitute EggBeaters™)
Grits or oatmeal
Whole-wheat toast with jelly

Hotcakes (3), hold butter,
  syrup on side
Golden brown waffle, hold butter,
  syrup on side
French toast, if grilled, not fried
  (hold butter, syrup on side)
Blueberry hotcakes, hold butter,
  syrup on side
Breakfast fruit
Blueberry or country morning
  muffins (2)

Margarine is served; butter is available upon request. Low-calorie syrup is available. EggBeaters™ can be substituted for eggs for a small charge.

PUTTING IT ALL TOGETHER

Light Choice for Breakfast
(Low in calories, fat, and cholesterol)
Blueberry pancakes with 3 tbsp.
  low-calorie syrup (hold breakfast
  meat and split order)
Egg (1) scrambled
Orange juice (regular)

Nutrition Values:

Calories	422
Carbohydrate (gm.)	62
Protein (gm.)	12
Fat (gm.)	18
% calories from fat	36
Cholesterol mg.)	263*
Sodium (mg.)	964

High in cholesterol

Exchanges: 2 Starch/Breads, 1 Meat (medium), 2 Fruits, 2 Fats

Moderate Choice for Breakfast
(Moderate in calories, low in fat, cholesterol)
(Order a la carte)
Breakfast fruit bowl
Oatmeal, 1 cup
Milk, 2% (8 oz.)
Whole-wheat toast, 2 slices
Margarine, 1 pat
Jam (1 pkg.)

Nutrition Values:

Calories	593
Carbohydrate (gm.)	101
Protein (gm.)	22
Fat (gm.)	14
5 calories from fat	21
Cholesterol (mg.)	18
Sodium (mg.)	502

Exchanges: 4 Starch/Breads, 2 Fruits, 1 Milk (low-fat), 2 Fats

BOB EVANS FARMS (cont.)

Best Bets for Lunch or Dinner

Soups
Texas style chili, cup
Beef vegetable soup, cup or bowl
Salads
Fruit bowl
Chef salad
Grilled chicken salad
Taco salad without tortilla shell
  and sour cream
Sandwiches
Deluxe hamburger
Grilled chicken sandwich platter
Family favorites
Homestyle meatloaf
Grilled chicken
Charbroiled catfish
Charbroiled chicken breast

Homestyle
Vegetable dinner
Chicken-N-Noodles
Spaghetti and meat sauce
Side dishes
Dinner roll
Garden salad
Green beans
Black-eyed peas
Turnip greens
Long-grain and wild rice
Grilled vegetables
Applesauce
Cottage cheese
Baked potato
Glazed baby carrots

Sandwiches are served on multigrain buns. Margarine is served unless butter is requested.

PUTTING IT ALL TOGETHER

Light Choice for Lunch or Dinner
(Low in calories, fat, and cholesterol)
Order from side dishes or a la carte
Baked potato
Cottage cheese
Green beans with butter (1 pat)
Baked apples

Nutrition Values:
Calories 420
Carbohydrate (gm.) 68
Protein (gm.) 18
Fat (gm.) 9
% calories from fat 20
Cholesterol (mg.) 27
Sodium (mg.) 1025

Exchanges: 3 Starch/Breads, 1 Meat
(medium). 1 Vegetable, 1 Fruit, 1 Fat

Moderate Choice for Lunch or Dinner
(Moderate in calories, low in fat, cholesterol)
Chicken-N-Noodles
Dinner roll
Garden salad with 2 tbsp. French
  dressing on the side

Nutrition Values:
Calories 835
Carbohydrate (gm.) 96
Protein (gm.) 43
Fat (gm.) 31
% calories from fat 34
Cholesterol (mg.) 151
Sodium (mg.) 1276

Exchanges: 5 Starch/Breads, 3 Meats
(lean), 3 Vegetables, 4 Fats

(OUNTRY KITCHEN

Best Bets for Breakfast

Juices and fruits
Chilled orange, grapefruit, or
 tomato (regular)
Fresh fruit in season

Pancakes (butter and syrup on side)
Short stack (hold meat)
Blueberry pancakes (hold meat
 and fruit compote)

Country Classics
*Eggstro'dnaire™ breakfast
 (served with fresh fruit and muffin)
Waffles with fruit (hold meat)

Side orders
*Hot or cold cereal with fruit and
 muffin
*English muffin, dry with jam
*Toast, dry with jam
*Freshly baked muffin
Fresh fruit medley with muffin

*Right Choice™ items. These have less than 400 calories, less than 100 mg. cholesterol, and
less than 1,000 mg. sodium. Eggstro'dnaire can be substituted for eggs for small charge.*

PUTTING IT ALL TOGETHER

Light Choice for Breakfast
(Low in calories, fat, and cholesterol)
Eggstro'dnaire™ breakfast
 Scrambled eggs
 Fresh fruit
 Warm muffin with 1 pkg. jelly

Nutrition Values:

Calories	481
Carbohydrate (gm.)	59
Protein (gm.)	23
Fat (gm.)	20
% calories from fat	37
Cholesterol (mg.)	47
Sodium (mg.)	1113

Exchanges:
2 Starch/Breads, 2 Meats (medium,
2 Fruits, 2 Fats

Moderate Choice for Breakfast
(Moderate calories, low fat, cholesterol)
Bran flakes with milk (2%)
Fresh fruit
Freshly baked muffin (1)

Nutrition Values:

Calories	490
Carbohydrate (gm.)	80
Protein (gm.)	18
Fat (gm.)	16
% calories from fat	29
Cholesterol (mg.)	60
Sodium (mg.)	683

Exchanges:
3 Starch/Breads, 1 1/2 Fruits,
1 Milk (2%), 2 Fats

COUNTRY KITCHEN (cont.)

Best Bets for Lunch or Dinner

Soups
*Old Fashioned Calico Bean Soup®

Salads
*Grilled chicken breast salad
*Country chef's salad
*Fajita salad, beef or chicken (hold guacamole, sour cream, light on chips, heavy on salsa)

Sandwiches
*French dip
*Barbecued pork sandwich
*Chicken breast sandwich

*All-American hot sandwiches (roast beef, meatloaf, or turkey)
Garden top burger (hold mayo, try mustard)

Country suppers
*Herb grilled chicken
Barbecued chicken (take half home)
*Rainbow trout
Top sirloin steak (6 oz. uncooked weight), substitute vegetables or baked potato for onion rings
Stir-fry chicken or beef
Spaghetti with meat balls

Right Choice™ items. These have less than 400 calories, less than 100 mg. cholesterol, and less than 1,000 mg. sodium

PUTTING IT ALL TOGETHER

Light Choice for Lunch or Dinner
(Low in calories, fat, and cholesterol)
Old-Fashioned Calico Bean Soup®, cup
Rainbow trout (take half home)
Baked potato with 1 pat butter
Vegetable with lemon wedges
Dinner roll

Nutrition Values:

Calories	614
Carbohydrate (gm.)	82
Protein (gm.)	37
Fat (gm.)	17
% calories from fat	24
Cholesterol (mg.)	73
Sodium (mg.)	1733

Exchanges:
5 Starch/Breads, 3 Meats (lean)
1 Vegetable, 2 Fats

Moderate Choice for Lunch or Dinner
(Moderate in calories, low in fat, cholesterol)
Stir-fry beef with oriental vegetables and teriyaki sauce
Rice pilaf
Garden salad with 2 tsp. olive oil and 2 tbsp. vinegar on side
Dinner roll

Nutrition Values:

Calories	770
Carbohydrate (gm.)	85
Protein (gm.)	31
Fat (gm.)	36
% calories from fat	41
Cholesterol (mg.)	57
Sodium (mg.)	1661

Exchanges:
3 Starch/Breads, 3 Meats (medium),
4 Vegetables, 4 Fats

CRACKER BARREL OLD COUNTRY STORE

Best Bets for Breakfast

Pancakes n' Such
Maple pancakes (butter and syrup
  on side)
French toast, grilled
Egg in basket (hold meat)

Cereal n' Fruit
Oatmeal breakfast with apple
  bran muffins
Oatmeal with bananas or raisins

Oatmeal or grits n' muffin
Grits
Assorted cold cereal with bananas
  or raisins

Everyday favorites (smaller portions)
Eggstro'dnaire™
Muffin n' fruit
One egg and toast or biscuit
Apple bran muffins
Sourdough toast

Eggstro'dnaire™ can be substituted for eggs at no additional charge. Any egg orders can be prepared with just one egg. Margarine and salt substitute are available on request.

PUTTING IT ALL TOGETHER

Light Choice for Breakfast
(Low in calories, fat, and cholesterol)
Apple bran muffin
Fresh sliced banana
Milk (2%) 8 oz.

Nutrition Values:
Calories 575
Carbohydrate (gm.) 100
Protein (gm.) 19
Fat (gm.) 11
% calories from fat 20
Cholesterol (mg.) 18
Sodium (mg.) 323

Exchanges:
4 Starch/Breads, 2 Fruits, 1 Milk (2%),
1 Fat

Moderate Choice for Breakfast
(Moderate in calories, low in fat, cholesterol)
Oatmeal with raisins and 2 tbsp.
  brown sugar
Apple bran muffin with 1 pat
  margarine
Coffee with 2 tbsp. regular milk

Nutrition Values:
Calorie. 753
Carbohydrate (gm.) 143
Protein (gm.) 17
Fat (gm.) 13
% calories from fat 15
Cholesterol (mg.) 0
Sodium (mg.) 686

Exchanges:
7 Starch/Breads, 2 Fruits, 3 Fats

CRACKER BARRELL (cont.)

Best Bets for Lunch or Dinner

Salads n' Such
(dressing on side with vinegar
or lemon to augment)
Grilled chicken salad
Grilled ham salad
Small chef salad
Tossed salad
Baked potato and cup of soup
Small chef salad and soup
or baked potato
Soup n' Sandwich (whole wheat bread)
Soup du jour (if broth based)
Country ham
Pork barbecue
Sliced turkey breast

Grilled chicken tenderloin
Grilled catfish
Fancy Fixins
Grilled chicken tenderloin
Charbroiled pork chops
Grilled farm raised catfish fillets
Country ham steak (choose baked
potato and tossed salad or vegetable
with corn muffin as accompani-
ments)

Country Dinner Plates
Country vegetable plate (choice
of 4 vegetables and corn bread)

PUTTING IT ALL TOGETHER

Light Choice for Lunch or Dinner
(Low in calories, fat, and cholesterol)
Country vegetable plate with
green beans, whole baby
carrots, pinto beans, and coleslaw
Corn muffin

Nutrition Values:
Calories 540
Carbohydrate (gm.) 78
Protein (gm.) 17
Fat (gm.) 19
% calories from fat 31
Cholesterol (mg.) 41
Sodium (mg.) 1596

Exchanges:
4 Starch/Breads, 3 Vegetables, 4 Fats

Moderate Choice for Lunch or Dinner
(Moderate in calories, low in fat, cholesterol)
Grilled farm raised catfish fillets
(take half home)
Corn
Tossed salad with 2 tbsp.
low-calorie Italian dressing on side
Biscuit
Milk, 8 oz. (2%)

Nutrition Values:
Calories 535
Carbohydrate (gm.) 50
Protein (gm.) .35
Fat (gm.) 23
% calories from fat 39
Cholesterol (mg.) 85
Sodium (mg.) 1469

Exchanges:
3 Starch/Breads, 3 Meats (lean),
1 Vegetable, 3 Fats

DENNY'S

Best Bets for Breakfast

	Calories	Carbohydrate (gm.)	Protein (gm.)	Fat (gm.)	Cholesterol (mg.)	Sodium (mg.)
Egg (1)	80	0	6	6	n/a	0
Pancake (1)	136	26	4	2	n/a	656
Biscuit (1)	217	35	4	7	n/a	800
Waffle (1)	261	35	6	10	n/a	62
Hash browns (4 oz.)	164	32	4	2	n/a	310
Ham slice (1)	156	1	14	7	n/a	1303
English muffin (whole)	137	26	6	1	n/a	n/a
Blueberry muffin (1)	309	42	4	14	n/a	190
Bagel (1)	240	47	9	1	n/a	450
Denver omelette (1)	567	11	47	27	n/a	1187

Additional side items for which no nutrition information is available: Grits, hot or cold cereal, applesauce, fresh fruit in season. EggBeaters™ and low-calorie syrup are available on request.

PUTTING IT ALL TOGETHER

Light Choice for Breakfast
(Low in calories, fat, and cholesterol)
Bagel with 1 tbsp. cream cheese
Grits with 1 tsp. butter
Orange juice (regular)

Nutrition Values:
Calories 549
Carbohydrate (gm.) 96
Protein (gm.) .14
Fat (gm.) 12
% calories from fat 19
Cholesterol (mg.) 26
Sodium (mg.) 951

Exchanges:
4 Starch/Breads, 2 Fruits, 2 Fats

Moderate Choice for Breakfast
(Moderate in calories, low in fat, cholesterol)
Denver omelette (request
   EggBeaters™, hold hash browns)
English muffin with 1 pkg. jam on side
Buttermilk pancakes
Margarine, 1 tsp.
Reduced-calorie syrup, 3 tbsp.
Bacon, 1 strip

Nutrition Values:
Calories 551
Carbohydrate (gm.) 73
Protein (gm.) 24
Fat (gm.) 18
% calories from fat 29
Cholesterol (mg.) 16
Sodium (mg.) 1170

Exchanges: 4 Starch/Breads, 2 Meats
(lean), 1 Vegetable, 1/2 Fruit, 2 Fats

DENNY'S (cont)

Best Bets for Lunch or Dinner

	Calories	Carbohydrate (gm.)	Protein (gm.)	Fat (gm.)	Cholesterol (mg.)	Sodium (mg.)
Soups						
Split pea, bowl	231	33	14	5	n/a	1519
Chicken noodle, bowl	105	15	4	3	n/a	1118
Beef barley, bowl	79	11	5	2	n/a	847
Chili, 4 oz.	169	15	10	8	n/a	677
Potato, bowl	248	38	5	9	n/a	1560
Salads						
Chef salad	492	13	36	20	n/a	1370
Taco salad (no shell)	514	35	31	20	n/a	2022
Chicken salad (no shell)	207	36	4	4	n/a	1762
Entrees						
Grilled chicken sandwich	439	40	27	12	n/a	413
Chicken strips (4)	290	21	23	12	50	670
Catfish	576	0	32	1	n/a	460
Stir-fry	328	5	36	11	n/a	109
Top sirloin steak	223	1	36	6	n/a	62
Liver with bacon and onions	334	10	40	15	n/a	516
Vegetables						
Peas (3 oz)	40	7	3	0	n/a	54
Carrots (3 oz.)	17	4	0	0	n/a	31
Corn (3 oz.)	63	15	2	1	n/a	37
Green beans (3 oz.)	13	3	1	0	n/a	22
Mashed potatoes (4 oz.)	74	15	2	0	n/a	302
Baked potato (medium)	90	21	3	0	n/a	7
Rice pilaf (3 oz.)	89	16	2	2	n/a	320

Soups, salads, and sides (salad dressing, vinegar, or lemon wedges on side)

Fresh garden salad with bowl of broth-based soup
Sandwich with bowl of soup or garden salad
California grilled chicken salad without tortilla shell and with reduced-calorie dressing or salsa
Taco salad without tortilla shell and with extra salsa
Chef salad (hold or light on cheese and olives)
Sandwich Specialties
Grilled chicken sandwich

Dinners
Mahimahi
Surf and Turf Slam
Stir-fry chicken and vegetables
Grilled catfish
Grilled breast of chicken (2 breasts)
Top sirloin steak
Liver with onions (hold bacon)

Sides
Garden salad
Bowl of chili
Bowl of soup, broth based

Dessert
Scoop of ice cream (single)
Apple or cherry pie (share)

PUTTING IT ALL TOGETHER

Light Choice for Lunch or Dinner
(Low in calories, fat, and cholesterol)
Grilled California chicken salad (hold tortilla, request 2 slices rye bread on side)
Salsa (4 tbsp.) to use as dressing

Nutrition Values:
Calories 414
Carbohydrate (gm.) 36
Protein (gm.) .41
Fat (gm.) 13
% calories from fat 28
Cholesterol (mg.) 96
Sodium (mg.) 671

Exchanges:
2 Starch/Breads, 4 Meats (lean),
2 Vegetables

Moderate Choice for Lunch or Dinner:
(Moderate in calories, low in fat, cholesterol)
Stir-fry chicken with vegetables
Rice pilaf
Garden salad with reduced-calorie Italian dressing
Apple pie (shared)

Nutrition Values:
Calories. 740
Carbohydrate (gm.) 81
Protein (gm.) .40
Fat (gm.) 28
% calories from fat 34
Cholesterol (mg.) 88
Sodium (mg.) 1037

Exchanges:
3 1/2 Starch/Breads, 4 Meats (lean)
2 Vegetables, 1 Fruit, 3 Fats

DUNKIN DONUTS

Best Bets

	Calories	Carbohydrate (gm.)	Protein (gm.)	Fat (gm.)	Cholesterol (mg.)	Sodium (mg.)
Muffins						
Blueberry	280	46	6	8	30	340
Bran with raisins	310	51	6	9	15	560
Corn	340	51	7	12	40	560
Banana nut	310	49	7	10	30	410
Apple N' Spice	300	52	6	8	25	360
Cranberry nut	290	44	6	9	25	360
Oat bran	330	50	7	11	0	450

Bagels with 1 oz. cream cheese on side
Plain, onion or cinnamon raisin
(No nutrition information available)

Beverages: Milk (2%), 8 oz.; Orange juice, 8 oz.

PUTTING IT ALL TOGETHER

Light Choice
(Low in calories, fat, and cholesterol)
Orange juice, 8 oz.
Raisin bran muffin
Coffee with 2 oz. regular milk

Nutrition Values:
Calories	436
Carbohydrate (gm.)	77
Protein (gm.)	8
Fat (gm.)	10
% calories from fat	21
Cholesterol (mg.)	19
Sodium (mg.)	575

Exchanges:
3 Starch/Breads, 2 Fruits, 2 Fats

Moderate Choice
(Moderate in calories, low in fat, cholesterol)
Onion bagel
Cream cheese (1 tbsp.)
Milk (2%), 8 oz.

Nutrition Values:
Calories	448
Carbohydrate (gm.)	65
Protein (gm.)	19
Fat (gm.)	12
% calories from fat	24
Cholesterol (mg.)	34
Sodium (mg.)	501

Exchanges:
2 Starch/Breads, 1 Milk (2%), 1 Fat

FRIENDLY'S

Best Bets for Breakfast

Rise n' Shine
One egg and bacon or sausage
One egg and home fries
French toast (grilled, not fried), 2 pieces
(hold bacon and sausage)
Buttermilk pancakes (2) (hold
bacon or sausage)
Bakery
Continental breakfast (muffin or
bagel)
Fresh baked muffin
Toasted bagel (cream cheese on side)
Thomas'® English muffin
Toast and Smuckers® jelly

Side orders
Seasonal fruit
Crisp cereal with milk
Two pancakes
Two slices French toast
Egg with toast

Juice
Orange, grapefruit, apple, tomato

EggBeaters™ may be substituted for eggs in any entree. Cholesterol-free margarine and low-fat (2%) milk and low-fat chocolate milk are available.

PUTTING IT ALL TOGETHER

Light Choice for Breakfast
(Low in calories, fat, and cholesterol)
French toast (2 pieces) with 3 tbsp.
regular pancake syrup
Seasonal fruit
Milk (2%), 8 oz

Nutrition Values:
Calories 692
Carbohydrate (gm.) 104
Protein (gm.) .21
Fat (gm.) 23
% calories from fat 30
Cholesterol (mg.s) 18
Sodium (mg.) 699

Exchanges:
4 Starch/Breads, 2 Fruits, 1 Milk (2%)
3 Fats

Moderate Choice for Breakfast
(Moderate in calories, low in fat, cholesterol)
Rise n' Shine Breakfast
Eggs (2) (scrambled, whites only)
Home fries
English muffin with 1 pkg. jam
Tomato juice
Coffee with 2 tbsp. regular milk

Nutrition Values:
Calories 546
Carbohydrate (gm.s) 75
Protein (gm.) .17
Fat (gm.) 21
% calories from fat 35
Cholesterol (mg.) 4
Sodium (mg.) 2042*
High in sodium
Exchanges:
4 Starch/Breads, 3 Vegetables, 4 Fats

FRIENDLY'S (cont.)

Best Bets for Lunch or Dinner

Salads
Seafood salad combo
Tuna salad combo
Chicken Choices
Chicken Hawaiian

Friendly's Classic Burgers
(5 oz. uncooked weight) with fresh garden salad instead of French fries
Italiano cheeseburger (hold cheese)
Hawaiian teriyaki burger (hold Canadian bacon)

Soup & Sides
Soup of the day (broth based)
Chili, cup or bowl
Soup and salad combo (dressing on side)

Baked potato (after 4 p.m.)
Rice pilaf
Hot vegetables
Cottage cheese
Sandwiches
Seafood pita pocket
Tuna pita pocket
Hamburger deluxe (hold mayo)

Platters (Choose from dinner roll, baked potato or rice pilaf, and hot vegetable)
Grilled barbecue chicken platter
Baked cod platter
Liver and onion (hold bacon)
Frozen yogurt

Vegetable oil is used, and low-fat (2%) regular and chocolate milk are available.

PUTTING IT ALL TOGETHER

Light Choice for Lunch or Dinner
(Low in calories, fat, and cholesterol)
Seafood pita pocket
Frozen yogurt (small scoop)

Nutrition Values:
Calories 495
Carbohydrate (gm.) 68
Protein (gm.) 23
Fat (gm.) 14
% calories from fat 26
Cholesterol (mg.) 37
Sodium (mg.) 1510

Exchanges: 2 Starch/Breads, 3 Meats (lean), 2 Fruits, 1 Fat

Moderate Choice for Lunch or Dinner
(Moderate in calories, low in fat, cholesterol)
Liver and onions platter
Baked potato with 1 pat butter
Vegetable (hot)
Dinner roll

Nutrition Values:
Calories 743
Carbohydrate (gm.) 79
Protein (gm.) .52
Fat (gm.) 25
% calories from fat 30
Cholesterol (mg.) 673*
Sodium (mg.) 1380
* Liver is high in cholesterol.

Exchanges: 3 Starch/Breads, 6 Meats (medium), 2 Vegetables, 1 Fat

HOWARD JOHNSON'S

Best Bets for Breakfast

Starters
Apple, tomato, or orange juice
(regular)
Fruit cup
Assorted cold cereals
Oatmeal with cinnamon apple and
raisins or sliced banana

Light Start (cereal, fresh fruit,
low-fat milk, wheat toast)

Club Breakfast (oatmeal, sliced
banana, English muffin)

Breakfast Combos
Fruit and yogurt platter with muffin

Strawberry hot cakes (hold whipped
cream and butter; syrup
on side)
Hot cakes (hold butter; syrup
on side)
Hot cakes and egg (hold butter;
syrup on side)

Sidelines
Grits (where available)
Muffin
Toast
English muffin
Bagel (cream cheese on side)
Low-fat yogurt

*EggBeaters™ may be substituted on any egg order. Olive oil, low-fat milk, and cholesterol-free
spread are available. Lighter portions at lighter prices are offered for patrons over age 60.*

PUTTING IT ALL TOGETHER

Light Choice for Breakfast
(Low in calories, fat, and cholesterol)
Oatmeal with 1/2 cup 2% milk
Sliced banana
English muffin with 2 tbsp. cream
cheese

Nutrition Values:
Calories 554
Carbohydrate (gm.) 87
Protein (gm.) 18
Fat (gm.) 16
% calories from fat 26
Cholesterol (mg.) 40
Sodium (mg.) 1025

Exchanges: 4 Starch/Breads, 1 Fruit,
3 Fats

Moderate Choice for Breakfast
(Moderate in calories, low in fat, cholesterol)
Fruit and yogurt platter
Muffin with 1 pat margarine

Nutrition Values:
Calories 753
Carbohydrate (gm.) 131
Protein (gm.) .19
Fat (gm.) 17
% calories from fat 20
Cholesterol (mg.) 22
Sodium (mg.) 343

Exchanges: 4 Starch/Bread, 4 Fruits, 1
Milk (2%), 2 Fats

HOWARD JOHNSON'S (cont.)

Best Bets for Lunch or Dinner

Appetizers
Soup, cup or bowl (broth based)
Chili (hold cheese)
Fruit cup
Vegetable sticks (with low-calorie
    dressing)
Super Salads (with low-calorie
    dressing on side)
Turkey oriental
Classic chef's (hold cheese)
Specialty Sandwiches
Vegetarian pocket
Turkey pajitas (fajitas)
Sandwich Favorites
Breast of turkey
Breast of turkey, half sandwich
    with dinner salad

Luncheon Selections
Mini-chef salad (dressing on side)
Chili and pasta (hold cheese)
Turkey cutlet (gravy on side)
Burgers and Franks
Hamburger topped with chili,
    mushrooms, onions, or sauerkraut
Poultry
Chicken stir-fry
Grilled chicken (choose
    cranberry-pineapple as topping)
Beef and more
Meat loaf
Pork chops (2 chops)
Pasta
Garden lasagna
Seafood
Broiled fish
Baked fish
Shrimp primavera

Dinners come with choice of two sides, including these healthier ones: Cup of broth-based soup, dinner salad, rice pilaf, hot vegetable, baked potato, lite ice milk, and yogurt

PUTTING IT ALL TOGETHER

Light Choice for Lunch or Dinner
(Low in calories, fat, and cholesterol)
Chili, bowl (no cheese, plenty
    of onions, 6 saltines)
Dinner salad with 2 tbsp. ranch
    dressing on side
Fruit cup

Nutrition Values:
Calories 460
Carbohydrate (gm.) 52
Protein (gm.) 23
Fat (gm.) 20
% calories from fat 39
Cholesterol (mg.) 45
Sodium (mg.) 1098

Exchanges: 2 Starch/Breads, 2 Meats
(medium), 1 Vegetable, 1 Fruit, 2 Fats

Moderate Choice for Lunch or Dinner
(Moderate in calories, low in fat, cholesterol)
Turkey Pajitas™ (fajitas)
Vegetable sticks
Frozen yogurt (small scoop)

Nutrition Values:
Calories 598
Carbohydrate (gm.) 80
Protein (gm.) 37
Fat (gm.) 15
% calories from fat 23
Cholesterol (mg.) 63
Sodium (mg.) 1431

Exchanges: 2 Starch/Breads
4 Meats (lean), 2 Vegetables, 2 Fruits,
1 Fat

HUDDLE HOUSE RESTAURANT

Best Bets for Breakfast

Golden waffle (butter and syrup
　　on side)

Pecan waffle (butter and syrup
　　on side)

Side orders
Bowl of hot grits
Raisin toast
Toast
Cereal with milk

Juices
Orange, tomato, grapefruit

No-cholesterol egg substitutes (scrambled only) and light syrup are available on request.

PUTTING IT ALL TOGETHER

Light Choice for Breakfast
(Low in calories, fat, and cholesterol)
Raisin toast
Grits with cheese (request light)
Grapefruit juice (medium)

Nutrition Values:
Calories 581
Carbohydrate (gm.) 94
Protein (gm.) .17
Fat (gm.) 16
% calories from fat 25
Cholesterol (mg.) 41
Sodium (mg.) 989

Exchanges:
4 Starch/Breads, 1 Meat (high fat),
2 Fruits, 1 Fat

Moderate Choice for Breakfast
(Moderate in calories, low in fat, cholesterol)
Golden waffle (1) with 3 tbsp. regular
　　pancake syrup
Orange juice (medium)

Nutrition Values:
Calories 644
Carbohydrate (gm.) 109
Protein (gm.) 12
Fat (gm.) 19
% calories from fat 27
Cholesterol (mg.) 68
Sodium (mg.) 716

Exchanges:
5 Starch/Breads, 2 Fruits, 3 Fats

HUDDLE HOUSE RESTAURANT (cont.)

Best Bets for Lunch or Dinner

Burger Plates
Hamburger plate (hold hash browns,
    French fries, substitute tossed salad)

Salads and Lighter Fare
Chef salad
Tossed green salad
Lettuce and tomato salad
Chef salad with grilled chicken

Sandwich plates (hold hash browns
    French fries, substitute tossed salad)
Grilled chicken sandwich plate
Grilled ham and cheese (toasted,
    not grilled)

**Dinners with tossed salad and light
    dressing** (hold hash browns
    or French fries)
Grilled chicken dinner
Hamburger steak dinner

Soups
Homestyle chili and crackers
Vegetable beef soup
Chicken noodle soup
Tomato soup

*Light dressing is available on request. All
fried products are cooked in 100% vegetable
oil.*

PUTTING IT ALL TOGETHER

Light Choice for Lunch or Dinner
(Low in calories, fat, and cholesterol)
Tomato soup, bowl
Chef salad with grilled chicken
    (hold cheese) and 2 tbsp.
    Thousand Island dressing on side
Saltines (6 crackers)

Nutrition Values:
Calories 517
Carbohydrate (gm.) 49
Protein (gm.) .36
Fat (gm.) 21
% calories from fat 37
Cholesterol (mg.) 193*
Sodium (mg.) 1877
    * *Egg yolk in salad is high in cholesterol.*

Exchanges:
2 Starch/Breads, 3 Meats (lean)
3 Vegetables, 2 Fats

Moderate Choice for Lunch or Dinner
(Moderate in calories, low in fat, cholesterol)
Chicken noodle soup, bowl
Saltines (6 crackers)
Grilled chicken dinner (hold French
    fries or hash browns)
Tossed salad with 2 tbsp.
    Italian dressing
Toasted bun (not grilled or buttered)

Nutrition Values:
Calories 613
Carbohydrate (gm.) 52
Protein (gm.) .46
Fat (gm.) 25
% calories from fat 37
Cholesterol (mg.) 108
Sodium (mg.) 2427*
            **Soup is high in sodium.*

Exchanges:
3 Starch/Breads, 4 Meats (lean)
1 Vegetable, 3 Fats

INTERNATIONAL HOUSE OF PANCAKES

Best Bets for Breakfast

Our Famous Pancakes (butter and syrup on side)
Old-fashioned buttermilk pancakes
Blueberry pancakes (hold blueberry compote)
Silver dollar pancakes
Harvest grain n' nut pancakes (plain or topped with strawberries)
International Specialties
French toast (grilled, not fried), with butter and syrup on side
Waffles
Golden waffle (butter and syrup on side)

Famous IHOP Omelettes
Omelette, build your own with 2 or 3 ingredients. (Best bets are ham, peppers and onions, chile salsa, mushrooms, Canadian bacon, broccoli, tomato)
Breakfast Sides
One egg, any style
Canadian-style bacon
English muffin (order dry with jelly)
Toast
Bagel (order dry with cream cheese on side)

PUTTING IT ALL TOGETHER

Light Choice for Breakfast
(Low in calories, fat, and cholesterol)
(From breakfast sides and juices)
Eggs (scrambled, 1 whole plus 1 white)
Bagel (dry with 1 tbsp. cream cheese on side)
Grapefruit juice
Coffee with 2 tbsp. regular milk

Nutrition Values:
Calories 516
Carbohydrate (gm.) 70
Protein (gm.) .21
Fat (gm.) 16
% calories from fat 28
Cholesterol (mg.) 239*
Sodium (mg.) 1032
High in cholesterol

Exchanges:
3 Starch/Breads, 2 Meats (medium)
2 Fruits, 1 Fat

Moderate Choice for Breakfast
(Moderate in calories, low in fat, cholesterol)
(Split meal or take half home)
Fajita omelette (chicken, onions, green peppers, cheese, salsa)
Harvest Grain n' Nut pancakes (1 1/2 pancakes) with 3 tbsp. regular syrup
Apple juice

Nutrition Values:
Calories 809
Carbohydrate (gm.) 99
Protein (gm.) 32
Fat (gm.) 32
% calories from fat 36
Cholesterol (mg.) 426*
Sodium (mg.) 2082*
* High in cholesterol and sodium.*

Exchanges:
4 Starch/Breads, 2 1/2 Meats (medium), 2 Fruits, 4 Fats

INTERNATIONAL HOUSE OF PANCAKES (cont.)

Best Bets for Lunch or Dinner

Sandwiches
Mushroom burger
Basic burger
Sliced turkey sandwich
Tuna salad sandwich
On the lighter side
Chef's Salad International
Tuna n' tomato

Dinner
Ham steak
Golden chicken (half, order
  with doggie bag)
Meat loaf
London broil (3 slices)
Spaghetti and meat sauce

Side orders
Bowl of soup of the day (broth based)
House dinner salad

PUTTING IT ALL TOGETHER

Light Choice for Lunch or Dinner
(Low in calories, fat, and cholesterol)
Tuna 'N' Tomato with lemon wedges
Bagel

Nutrition Values:
Calories 535
Carbohydrate (gm.) 55
Protein (gm.) .35
Fat (gm.) 21
% calories from fat 34
Cholesterol (mg.) 23
Sodium (mg.) 1182

Exchanges:
3 Starch/Breads, 3 Meats (lean),
2 Vegetables, 2 Fats

Moderate Choice for Lunch or Dinner
(Moderate in calories, low in fat, cholesterol)
London broil (3 slices)
Crisp green salad with 2 tbsp.
  French dressing and vinegar on side
Baked potato (1 tbsp. sour cream
  on side)
Steamed vegetable
Dinner roll with 1 pat butter

Nutrition Values:
Calories 641
Carbohydrate (gm.) 69
Protein (gm.) .36
Fat (gm.) 26
% calories from fat 36
Cholesterol (mg.) 99
Sodium (gm.) 1074

Exchanges:
4 Starch/Breads, 4 Meats (lean),
1 Vegetable, 2 Fats

JB'S

Best Bets for Breakfast

Breakfast Buffet (choose carefully from cereal, fresh fruit, juices, breads, muffins)

Griddle and Iron (a la carte with butter and syrup on side)
Belgian waffle
Pancake stack
French toast (grilled, not fried)

Omelettes
Western made with egg substitute (share)

Freshly baked muffins

Low-cholesterol egg substitute is available.

PUTTING IT ALL TOGETHER

Light Choice for Breakfast
(Low in calories, fat, and cholesterol)
From the breakfast buffet:
  Raisin bran cereal
  Milk (2%), 8 oz.
  Fresh fruit
  Bran muffin

Nutrition Values:
Calories 511
Carbohydrate (gm.) 87
Protein (gm.) .18
Fat (gm.) 16
% calories from fat 27
Cholesterol (mg.) 60
Sodium (mg.) 771

Exchanges:
3 Starch/Breads, 2 Fruits,
1 Milk (2%), 1 Fat

Moderate Choice for Breakfast
(Moderate in calories, low in fat, cholesterol)
French toast (a la carte) with
  3 tbsp. regular syrup
Apple juice

Nutrition Values:
Calories 776
Carbohydrate (gm.) 121
Protein (gm.) .17
Fat (gm.) 25
% calories from fat 29
Cholesterol (mg.) 0
Sodium (mg.) 1396

Exchanges:
6 Starch/Breads, 2 Fruits, 4 Fats

FUN FOOD FACTS

• More than one of every 5 people over 8 years of age eats a commercially prepared breakfast at least once a week. *Restaurants USA, September, 1991.*

JB'S (cont.)

Best Bets for Lunch and Dinner

All you can eat soup and salad bar (choose carefully)

Homestyle Burgers
All-American Cheeseburger (hold cheese, request coleslaw)

Sandwiches
French dip
Turkey breast stack
Bacon, lettuce, and tomato (hold mayonnaise, request plain bread, not grilled)

Steak and Seafood
Chicago-style choice steak, 6 oz. uncooked weight (hold bacon)
North Atlantic cod almondine

Chicken sandwich (hold cheese and mayonnaise)

Garden Fresh
Soup and salad bar
Steamed veggies (hold tortilla shell)

Country platters
Ranch-style chopped steak
Homestyle meat loaf

Pasta
Bayou Cajun chicken (substitute plain roll for Parmesan toast)
Mama's Original Spaghetti (substitute plain roll for Parmesan toast)

Chicken
Chicken stir-fry

PUTTING IT ALL TOGETHER

Light Choice for Lunch or Dinner
(Low in calories, fat, and cholesterol)
1/2 ham sandwich (hold cheese, have mustard on side)
Salad bar with 2 tbsp. French dressing and vinegar (See page 4 for best salad bar choices.)

Nutrition Values:
Calories 498
Carbohydrate (gm.) 53
Protein (gm.) 29
Fat (gm.) 22
% calories from fat 39
Cholesterol (mg. 49
Sodium (mg.) 2166*

Ham is high in sodium. Choose half of a turkey sandwich if sodium is a problem.

Exchanges:
2 Starch/Breads, 3 Meats (medium)
3 Vegetables, 1 Fat

Moderate Choice for Lunch or Dinner
(Moderate in calories, low in fat, cholesterol)
"Bayou" Cajun Chicken (chicken, noodles, and vegetables)
Garden salad with 2 tbsp. blue cheese salad dressing on side
Dinner roll (instead of Parmesan toast)

Nutrition Value:
Calories 889
Carbohydrate (gm.) 99
Protein (gm.) .54
Fat (gm.) 32
% calories from fat 32
Cholesterol (mg.) 181*
Sodium (mg.) 1179
High in cholesterol.

Exchanges:
5 Starch/Breads, 4 Meats (lean),
3 Vegetables, 4 Fats

MARIE CALLENDER'S

Best Bets for Lunch and Dinner

Soups
Hearty vegetable
Split pea and smoked ham
Old-fashioned navy bean
Chicken noodle
Salads
Salad bar and soup
Chicken sesame salad
Grilled chicken caesar (light on
   dressing)
Juicy burgers
Marie's Original
Lighter Side
Grilled lemon chicken
Grilled halibut
Almond ginger stir-fry
Vegetable platter (hold cheese)
Oriental stir-fry

Sandwiches (choose salad bar
   and soup instead of French fries)
French dip
Turkey stack
Old-fashioned meatloaf sandwich
   (French roll)
Homestyle Classics
Teriyaki chicken grill
Marie's baked meatloaf
Marie's homestyle pot roast
Lasagna
Sicilian meatballs and spaghetti
Marie's Favorites
Bread Basket Stew
Chili and cornbread
Pies
Apple, lite
Fresh peach, lite

Menu lists several "on the lighter side" items.

PUTTING IT ALL TOGETHER

Light Choice
(Low in calories, fat, and cholesterol)
Vegetable platter with cheese sauce
Cornbread (1 piece)
Fresh peach pie, lite (split)

Nutrition Values:
Calories. 650
Carbohydrate (gm.) 98
Protein (gm.) 22
Fat (gm.) 22
% calories from fat 30
Cholesterol (mg.) 27
Sodium (mg.) 1708

Exchanges: 4 Starch/Breads, 3 Vegetables, 1 1/2 Fruits, 4 Fats

Moderate Choice
(Moderate in calories, low in fat, cholesterol)
Chicken sesame salad (hold wontons,
   light on Chinese noodles) with
   3 tbsp. light Oriental dressing on side
Corn bread (1 piece)

Nutrition Values:
Calories 831
Carbohydrate (gm.) 75
Protein (gm.) .40
Fat (gm.) 33
% calories from fat 40
Cholesterol (mg.) 72
Sodium (mg.) 1959

Exchanges: 4 Starch/Breads, 4 Meats
(lean), 2 Vegetables, 1 Fruit, 4 Fats

PERKINS

Best Bets for Breakfast

Traditional Omelettes (split or prepare with egg substitute)
Denver omelette
Seafood omelette

Pancakes, waffles, etc. (butter and syrup on side)
Short stack (3 pancakes)
Potato pancakes (hold bacon)
Harvest cakes (3)
Belgian waffle
Authentic French toast, grilled, not fried

Hearty Extras
Oatmeal and muffin
Breakfast cereal and milk
Blueberry, bran, or corn muffin
Toast
English muffin
Fresh fruit

Egg substitute and reduced-calorie syrup are available. Margarine blend is served. Lite and Healthy items are marked on menus.

PUTTING IT ALL TOGETHER

Light Choice for Breakfast
(Low in calories, fat, and cholesterol)
Harvest cakes (3), with butter and 2 tbsp. reduced-calorie syrup on side
Fresh fruit, 1 cup
Coffee with 2 tbsp. regular milk

Nutrition Values:

Calories. 403
Carbohydrate (gm.) 86
Protein (gm.) .12
Fat (gm.) 10
% calories from fat 19
Cholesterol (mg.) 85
Sodium (mg.) 981

Exchanges: 4 Starch/Breads, 2 Fruits, 2 Fats

Moderate Choice for Breakfast
(Moderate in calories, low in fat, cholesterol)
Denver omelette (order with Eggstro'dinaire® egg substitute) with turkey, ham, onions, celery, and green peppers with cheese sauce —light on sauce)
Bran muffin
Chilled fruit cup

Nutrition Values:

Calories 624
Carbohydrate (gm.) 58
Protein (gm.) .40
Fat (gm.) 25
% calories from fat 41
Cholesterol (mg.) 103
Sodium (mg.) 1879

Exchanges: 2 Starch/Breads, 4 Meats (medium), 1 Fruit, 2 Vegetables, 2 Fats

Best Bets for Lunch and Dinner

Specialty Salads
Grilled lemon chicken (hold
   bread bowl)
Grilled teriyaki chicken (hold
   bread bowl)
Seafood chef (hold bread bowl)
Taco (hold tortilla shell)
Mini chef with muffin
Salad bar (choose carefully)

Sandwiches
Hamburger
French dip
Cajun chicken pita
Lemon chicken pita

Deluxe Dinners
Teriyaki chicken
Cajun chicken
Lemon pepper chicken
Teriyaki steak (split) and salad bar
Homestyle meatloaf
Orange roughy
Chicken marinara

*Some menu items are marked Lite and
Healthy. Some selections are available in
smaller portions for seniors.*

PUTTING IT ALL TOGETHER

Light Choice for Lunch or Dinner
(Low in calories, fat, and cholesterol)
Mini chef salad with 2 tbsp.
   reduced-calorie French dressing
   and extra lemon wedges on side
Muffin
Margarine (1 pat)
Milk (2%), 8 oz.

Nutrition Values:
Calories 533
Carbohydrate (gm.) 50
Protein (gm.) 37
Fat (gm.) 22
% calories from fat 37
Cholesterol (mg.) 106
Sodium (mg.) 1273

Exchanges: 2 Starch/Breads, 3 Meats
(medium), 2 Vegetables, 1 Milk

Moderate Choice for Lunch or Dinner
(Moderate in calories, low in fat and cholesterol)
Orange roughy, grilled (split)
Vegetable
Dinner roll
Baked potato (1/2) with 1 tbsp.
   cottage cheese
Salad bar with 2 tbsp. Italian dressing
   and vinegar (See page 6 for salad
   bar information.)

Nutrition Values:
Calories 751
Carbohydrate (gm.) 84
Protein (gm.) 35
Fat (gm.) 34
% calories from fat 40
Cholesterol (mg.) 25
Sodium (mg.) 1672

Exchanges: 4 Starch/Breads, 3 Meats
(lean), 3 Vegetables, 4 Fats

PO FOLKS

Best Bets

Appetizers and Salads
Cup of broth-based soup
Garden patch salad
Grilled chicken salad (hold cheese)
Cottage cheese and tomatoes
Soup (broth based) and salad
Homestyle dinners (with 2 vegetables and breadstick or cornbread)
Chicken n' dumplings
Pot roast dinner
Mason Dixon meatloaf dinner
Pork chop dinner (one chop, broiled)
Favorites from grill (with 2 vegetables and breadstick or cornbread)
Fish dinner
Rainbow trout
Chicken breast (take 1/2 home)
Grilled liver and onions

Homestyle vegetables, etc.
Vegetable platter (choice of 4 vegetables with breadstick or cornbread)
Sliced tomatoes
Corn on the cob
Turnip greens
Green beans
Red beans and rice
Black-eyed peas
Baked potatoes
Cabbage
Seafood favorites (choose 2 vegetables and request breadstick instead of hush puppies)
Catfish fillet dinner
Fillet of fish dinner (small size)
Dessert
Vanilla ice cream (1 scoop)

PUTTING IT ALL TOGETHER

Light Choice
(Low in calories, fat, and cholesterol)
Cottage cheese and tomato salad
Garden patch salad with 2 tsp. olive oil and vinegar
Cornbread (1 piece)

Nutrition Values:
Calories 464
Carbohydrate (gm.) 49
Protein (gm.) 23
Fat (gm.) 21
% calories from fat 41
Cholesterol (mg.) 19
Sodium (mg.) .822

Exchanges: 2 Starch/Breads, 2 Meats (lean), 3 Vegetables, 3 Fats

Moderate Choice
(Moderate in calories, low in fat, cholesterol)
Pork chop dinner (one chop, broiled, hold gravy)
Vegetables (3)
Turnip greens, red beans and rice
Corn on the cob
Corn bread (1 piece)

Nutrition Values:
Calories 977
Carbohydrate (gm.) 96
Protein (gm.) 44
Fat (gm.) 47
% calories from fat 43
Cholesterol (mg.) 106
Sodium (mg.) 1818

Exchanges: 5 Starch/Breads, 4 Meats (medium), 2 Vegetables, 5 Fats

SHONEY'S

Best Bets for Breakfast

Breakfast Bar
Eggs, muffins, biscuits, grits, fresh fruit
Breakfast Combination
One egg, any style, with grits,
toast, and jam

Side orders
Pancakes (butter, syrup on side)
Toast and jam

PUTTING IT ALL TOGETHER

Light Choice for Breakfast
(Low in calories, fat, and cholesterol)
Biscuit with 1 pkg. jam
Grits with 1 tsp. butter
Fresh fruit
Coffee with 1 tbsp. regular milk

Nutrition Values:

Calories .... .445
Carbohydrate (gm.) .... .69
Protein (gm.) 8
Fat (gm.) .... .16
% calories from fat .... .32
Cholesterol (mg.) .... .15
Sodium (mg.) 946

Exchanges: 3 Starch/Breads, 2 Fruits,
2 Fats

Moderate Choice for Breakfast
(Moderate in calories, low in fat, cholesterol)
Pancakes (3) with 2 tbsp. light syrup
Bacon, 1 strip
Sausage, 1 link
Fresh fruit, 1/2 cup
Coffee with 2 tbsp. regular milk

Nutrition Values:

Calories 436
Carbohydrate (gm.) 71
Protein (mg.) 12
Fat (gm.) 11
% calories from fat 24
Cholesterol (mg.) .... .20
Sodium (mg.) 1167

Exchanges: 3 Starch/Breads, 1 1/2
Fruits, 2 Fats

Best Bets for Lunch of Dinner

	Calories	Carbohydrate (gm.)	Protein (gm.)	Fat (gm.)	Cholesterol (mg.)	Sodium (mg.)
Soup						
LightSide (average of soups)	73	11	3	4	503	n/a
LightSide dinners *(includes salad, low-calorie dressing, and soup)*						
Baked fish	170	2	35	1	83	1641
Charbroiled chicken	239	1	39	7	85	592
Lasagna	297	45	8	10	26	870
Spaghetti	248	32	12	8	28	194

SHONEY'S (cont.)

Best Bets for Lunch or Dinner

Soup, Salad, and Fruit Bar
Sandwiches/Burgers
Charbroiled chicken sandwich
All-American burger (5 oz.
uncooked weight)

Dinners
Charbroiled chicken
Hawaiian chicken
Sirloin (5 oz., uncooked weight)
Baked fish
Old-fashioned burger

LightSide*
Light charbroiled shrimp
Light charbroiled chicken
Light lasagna
Light spaghetti
Light baked fish
Light beef patty

* LightSide offerings are less than 500 calories when eaten with a garden salad and low-calorie dressing.

PUTTING IT ALL TOGETHER

Light Choice for Lunch or Dinner
(Low in calories, fat, and cholesterol)
LightSide soup
LightSide lasagna
Hamburger bun, hoagie roll (on side)
Salad bar with 2 tbsp. low-calorie
dressing on side (See page 6
for salad bar information.)

Nutrition Values:

Calories	593
Carbohydrate (gm.)	99
Protein (gm.)	21
Fat (gm.)	13
% calories from fat	19
Cholesterol (mg.)	30
Sodium (mg.)	1974

Exchanges:
4 Starch/Breads, 2 Meats (medium),
3 Vegetables, 1 Fat

Moderate Choice for Lunch or Dinner
(Moderate in calories, low in fat, cholesterol)
Hawaiian chicken with grilled
pineapple and sweet and sour sauce
Rice
Salad bar with 2 tbsp. Thousand Island
dressing on side (See page 6
for salad bar information.)
Fruit from fruit bar (1 cup)

Nutrition Values:

Calorie	836
Carbohydrate (gm.)	112
Protein (gm.)	49
Fat (gm.)	24
% calories from fat	26
Cholesterol (mg.)	106
Sodium (mg.)	1593

Exchanges:
5 Starch/Breads, 4 Meats (lean),
3 Vegetables, 1 1/2 Fruits, 2 Fats

VILLAGE INN

Best Bets for Breakfast

Low-fat, low-cholesterol, and low-sodium breakfasts
Mushroom and cheese omelette
Granola and fruit with yogurt and blueberry muffin
Chicken and cheese omelette
Fresh veggie omelette
Low-cholesterol fruit and nut pancakes (3)

Pancakes, Waffles, and French Toast (butter and syrup on side)
Strawberry and whipped cream (order fresh strawberries only)
Short stack buttermilk pancakes
Fruit Belgian waffle with fresh strawberries
French toast, grilled, not fried
Light breakfast (1 egg, 3 pancakes)

Margarine is regularly served. Low-cholesterol eggs available on request. Menu lists lighter breakfasts.

PUTTING IT ALL TOGETHER

Light Choice for Breakfast
(Low in calories, fat, and cholesterol)
Fresh veggie omelette made with low-cholesterol eggs and onions, green pepper, tomato, mushrooms, zucchini, and skim mozzarella cheese, topped with salsa
Fresh fruit, 1/2 cup
Whole-wheat toast, 2 slices
Jam, 1 tbsp.
Coffee with 2 tbsp. regular milk

Nutrition Values:
Calories 460
Carbohydrate (gm.) 51
Protein (gm.) 29
Fat (gm.) 17
% calories from fat 33
Cholesterol (mg.) 21
Sodium (mg.) .684

Exchanges:
2 Starch/Breads, 3 Meats (medium), 1 Vegetable, 1 Fruit

Moderate Choice for Breakfast
(Moderate in calories, low in fat, cholesterol)
Egg, 1 poached
Buttermilk pancakes (3) with 3 tbsp. regular syrup
Bacon (2 strips, extra crispy)

Nutrition Values:
Calories 617
Carbohydrate (gm.) 90
Protein (gm.) .20
Fat (gm.) 21
% calories from fat 31
Cholesterol (mg.) 324*
Sodium (mg.) 1274
* High in cholesterol

Exchanges:
5 Starch/Breads, Meat (medium), 1 Fruit, 3 Fats

VILLAGE INN (cont.)

Best Bets for Lunch and Dinner

Garden Fresh salads (with dressing on side and extra vinegar or lemon wedges)
Cobb salad (hold bacon)
Tuna salad
Shrimp salad (cocktail sauce on side)
Garden Grand Salad (light on cheese)
Mexican salad (hold cheese, sour cream, tortilla chips; request extra salsa)
Village Inn Chef salad
Inn Burgers/Sandwiches
All-American Burger
Avocado Swiss chicken sandwich (hold cheese)
Hot roast beef sandwich

Village Inn Entrees
Chicken tenderloins Italiano
Center cut pork chops
Grilled sole
Fish fillet
On the Lighter Side
Mini tuna salad
Light grilled fish
Mini chef salad
Half sandwich and soup
On the side
Cottage cheese
Dinner salad
Soup, cup or bowl
Chili, cup or bowl

PUTTING IT ALL TOGETHER

Light Choice for Lunch or Dinner
(Low in calories, fat, and cholesterol)
Garden Grand Salad (light on cheese) with 2 tsp. oil and vinegar on side
Bagel

Nutrition Values:
Calories 489
Carbohydrate (gm.) 57
Protein (gm.) .18
Fat (gm.) 23
% calories form fat 42
Cholesterol (mg.) 30
Sodium (mg.) 705

Exchanges: 3 Starch/Breads, 2 Vegetables, 4 Fats

Moderate Choice for Lunch or Dinner
(Moderate in calories, low in fat, cholesterol)
Grilled sole (take half home)
Baked potato with 2 tbsp. sour cream
Garden vegetables
Dinner bread (1 slice)
Tossed salad with 2 tbsp.
    Thousand Island dressing on side
Bowl fresh fruit

Nutrition Values:
Calories 657
Carbohydrate (gm.) 91
Protein (gm.) 28
Fat (gm.) 24
% calories from fat 33
Cholesterol (mg.) 62
Sodium (mg.) 1036

Exchanges: 4 Starch/Breads, 2 Meats (lean), 2 Vegetables, 1 Fruit, 3 Fat

WAFFLE HOUSE

Best Bets for Breakfast

A La Carte
Waffle with light syrup (butter
   and syrup on side)
One egg with toast and jelly

Raisin toast
Bowl of grits
Cereal with milk (2%)

Lite syrup available on request.

PUTTING IT ALL TOGETHER

Light Choice for Breakfast
(Light in calories, fat, and cholesterol)
Bran Flakes (1-oz. box) with 8 oz.
   2% milk
Banana
Coffee with 2 tbsp. regular milk

Nutrition Values:
Calories 285
Carbohydrate (gm.) 49
Protein (gm.) .13
Fat (gm.) 7
% calories from fat 22
Cholesterol (mg.) 22
Sodium (mg.) 358

Exchanges:
1 1/2 Starch/Bread, 1 Fruit, 1 Milk
(low-fat)

Moderate Choice for Breakfast
(Moderate in calories, low in fat, cholesterol)
(Order a la carte)
Waffle with 3 tbsp. regular syrup
Ham
Milk (2%), 8 oz.

Nutrition Values:
Calories 735
Carbohydrate (gm.) 95
Protein (gm.) 31
Fat (gm.) 26
% calories from fat 32
Cholesterol (mg.) 103
Sodium (mg.) 769

Exchanges:
5 Starch/Breads, 2 Meats, 1 Fruit,
3 Fats

WAFFLE HOUSE (cont.)

Best Bets for Lunch or Dinner

Salad
Salad supreme with chicken
Bert's salad

The Light Corner
Chef salad
Vegetable beef soup and fresh
    tossed salad

Sandwiches
Hamburger
Chicken sandwich
Chop steak sandwich
Ham, lettuce, and tomato

PUTTING IT ALL TOGETHER

Light Choice for Lunch or Dinner
(Low in calories, fat, and cholesterol)
Vegetable beef soup with 6
    saltine crackers
Fresh tossed salad with 1 tbsp.
    blue cheese dressing on side
Milk (2%) 8 oz.

Nutrition Values:
Calories 303
Carbohydrate (gm.) 40
Protein (gm.) 16
Fat (gm.) 9
% calories from fat 27
Cholesterol (mg.) 31
Sodium (mg.) 1485

Exchanges: 2 Starch/Bread,
1 Vegetable, 1 Milk (2%),
1 Fat

Moderate Choice for Lunch or Dinner
(Moderate in calories, low in fat, cholesterol)
Chicken sandwich plate (hold
    mayo and hash browns)
Large tossed salad with 1 tbsp.
    blue cheese dressing and vinegar
    on the side
Saltines (6)
Milk (2%), 8 oz.

Nutrition Values:
Calories 492
Carbohydrate (gm.) 48
Protein (gm.) 30
Fat (gm.) 20
% calories from fat 37
Cholesterol (mg.) 73
Sodium (mg.) 801

Exchanges: 2 Starch/Bread,
1 Vegetable, 3 Meat (lean), 1 Milk (2%),
2 Fats

FUN FOOD FACTS

• **The largest omelette prepared in the U.S. was 706 feet, 8 inches in diameter. It was made with 54,763 eggs and 531 pounds of cheese in a skillet 30 feet in diameter.** *Guiness Book of Records, 1992.*

MEXICAN RESTAURANTS

Mexican food is America's favorite ethnic cuisine. Mexican restaurant chains come in two varieties—fast food and table service. Fast food chains favor short menus dedicated to quick and tasty tacos, burritos, etc. Table service restaurants whet your appetite with margaritas and chips and salsa for starters. Fajitas, chimichangas, and enchiladas line the rest of the menus. Entrees are often complemented with Mexican rice and refritos frijoles (refried beans). Unfortunately, meals are often piled with high-fat and calorie-dense items such as cheese, sour cream, and guacamole. Sodium can also skyrocket. Bean dishes provide healthy carbohydrates and much needed fiber, but they're high in sodium. Even the low-fat spicy sauces are often loaded with sodium.

Though the picture looks less than ideal for the health conscious—have no fear. Get back to basics and stick with grains, vegetables, and beans. Keep portions light, avoid high fat preparations and avoid the add ons—cheese, sour cream, and guacamole. Balance the added fat and salt of Mexican food by eating light at other meals.

Healthier Mexican eating is possible—that is, if you are willing to read the menu carefully, take advantage of nonfried items, order a la carte, and choose next-to-no-calorie hot and spicy sauces.

Nutrition Pros

■ An entree need not be ordered. Choosing from appetizers and side items helps you control portions.
■ Mixing dishes is quite acceptable. The result? More tastes and less food.
■ High-fat items are added on selections, not mixed in, so special requests to hold, use less, or serve on the side are easily handled.
■ Hot and spicy sauces add zest without the fat and calories of sour cream, cheese, dressings, and other toppings.
■ Mexican cuisine is naturally low in protein (chicken and beef) and higher in carbohydrates (beans, rice, tortillas).

Nutrition Cons

■ Fried items seem unavoidable: chips, tacos, chimichangas, tortilla shells.
■ High-fat toppings such as sour cream, cheese, and guacamole seem to coat every dish.
■ Cheese is a mainstay, either shredded, melted, or sauced.
■ Healthy appetizers are scarce.
■ Fruit is nowhere to be found.
■ Vegetables are few and far between, especially in fast food.
■ Healthy high-fiber beans are often refried.

CHI CHI'S

Best Bets

Appetizers
Mexican pizza (share or order as entree)

Fresh & Light
Taco salad, beef or chicken (hold shell and cheese, request soft flour tortillas and extra salsa)

Seafood salad (hold shell and cheese, request guacamole on the side, soft flour tortillas, and extra salsa)

Grilled chicken salad

Southwest chicken (request dressing on the side)

Mexican dinner salad (hold shell and cheese, request extra pico de gallo)

San Antonio chili (hold sour cream and cheese, request chopped onions or pico de gallo)

Burros Favorites
Chili burro (hold cheese, request pico de gallo as substitute for refried beans)

Chicken burro suprema (hold sour cream, request pico de gallo as substitute for refried beans)

Char-Broiled
Chajitas® (Chi-Chi's name for fajitas)*

Steak, chicken, or shrimp (combo of 2, single)

Pollo magnifico (request salsa or hot sauce as salad dressing

Halibut (hold butter on top, request salad dressing on the side)

Create Your Own Combinations
Taco, soft flour tortilla with beef, chicken, or seafood

Sides
Spanish rice
Soft flour tortillas (2)
Diablo sauce
Pico de gallo

Luncheons
Chicken sandwich (request the substitution of rice for fries)

Chajitas® (hold sour cream and guacamole)

Taco salad (hold shell and cheese)

Available in two styles: ranch (hold guacamole and sour cream, request extra salsa or pico de gallo) and hacienda style (request salad dressing on the side)

Chi Chi's uses only 100 percent vegetable oil and provides a description of sauces in the menu.

PUTTING IT ALL TOGETHER

Light Choice
(Low in calories, fat, and cholesterol)
San Antonio chili (hold cheese, request raw onions)
Flour tortillas (2)
Mexican dinner salad, Tex Mex style (hold cheese, request salsa on the side as salad dressing)
Milk (2%) 8 oz.

Nutrition Values:
Calories 566
Carbohydrate (gm.) 79
Protein (gm) .34
Fat (gm.) 16
% calories from fat 25
Cholesterol (mg.) 58
Sodium (mg.) 1023

Exchanges:
5 Starch/Breads, 2 Meats (medium) ,
2 Vegetables , 1 Fat

Moderate Choice
(Moderate in calories, low in fat and cholesterol)
(Split both meals)
Seafood salad (hold guacamole, tortilla shell, request light on cheese)
Salsa (use for dressing)
Tortillas (2), side order
Chicken Burro Suprema (hold sour cream, request light on cheese)
Spanish rice (1/2), on side
Refried beans (1/2), on side

Nutrition Values:
Calories 858
Carbohydrate (gm.) 94
Protein (gm.) 51
Fat (gm.) 33
% calories from fat 35
Cholesterol (mg.) 126
Sodium (mg.) 2603*
* High in sodium

Exchanges:
5 Starch/Breads, 3 Vegetabes, 4 Meats (medium), 2 Fats

FUN FOOD FACTS

• From 1986 to 1990, the number of people who ate at fast food Mexican restaurants increased 42 percent over all other fast food restaurants. *Restaurants and Institutions, March 25, 1992.*

• The number of Mexican entrees offered in all types of restaurants has swelled 180 percent. *Restaurants and Institutions, March 25, 1992.*

• Chili con carne, Spanish for "chili with meat," is a mixture of diced or ground beef and chili powder. It originated in the Lone Star State where it is commonly called a "blow of red." Texans also consider it a crime to add beans to the mixture. *Food Lover's Companion, 1990.*

DEL TACO

Best Bets

	Calories	Carbohydrate (gm.)	Protein (gm.)	Fat (gm.)	Cholesterol (mg.)	Sodium (mg.)
Breakfast burrito	256	30	9	11	90	409
Quesadilla	257	26	11	12	30	455
Hamburger	231	26	11	8	29	649
Cheeseburger	284	26	14	13	42	852
Combination burrito	413	46	21	17	49	1035
Big Del burrito	453	49	22	20	59	1047
Del beef burrito	440	43	23	20	63	878
Deluxe chicken fajita burrito	435	41	22	22	84	944
Red burrito	235	32	10	8	17	656
Red burrito, large	342	46	14	11	22	1149
Green burrito	229	32	9	8	15	714
Green burrito, large	330	46	14	11	22	1149
Chicken burrito	264	32	13	10	36	771
Soft taco	146	17	5	6	16	223
Regular soft taco	211	19	9	10	32	320
Deluxe chicken fajita taco	211	18	11	10	53	492

Sides

Beans 'n cheese	122	17	7	7	9	890
French fries	242	32	3	11	0	136

Sauces

Guacamole (2 tbsp.)	60	2	1	6	0	130
Salsa (4 tbsp.)	14	3	1	0	1	308
Hot sauce (1 tbsp.)	2	1	0	0	0	38

Beverages

Orange juice	83	20	1	0	0	19
Milk, low fat (1%)	126	15	10	3	12	152

No lard is used in beans and tortillas, and products are fried in 100 percent cholesterol-free vegetable shortening.

PUTTING IT ALL TOGETHER

Light Choice
(Low in calories, fat, and cholesterol)

Deluxe chichen fajita taco
Soft taco
Salsa (4 tbsp.)
Milk (1%) 8 oz.

Nutrition Values:
Calories 497
Carbohydrate (gm.) 53
Protein (gm.) .27
Fat (gm.) 19
% calories from fat 34
Cholesterol (mg.) 82
Sodium (mg.) 1176

Exchanges:
2 Starch/Breads, 2 Meats (lean),
2 Vegetables, 1 Milk (1%), 1 Fat

Moderate Choice
(Moderate in calories, low in fat and cholesterol)

Red burrito
Green burrito
Beans 'n cheese
Hot sauce (2 packets)

Nutrition Values:
Calories 650
Carbohydrate (gm.) 85
Protein (gm.) 27
Fat (gm.) 29
% calories from fat 40
Cholesterol (mg.) 41
Sodium (mg.) 2466*
* High in sodium

Exchanges:
5 Starch/Breads, 2 Meats (medium),
3 Fats

EL CHICO

Best Bets

Soup and Salads

Tortilla soup (hold cheese)

Chicken fajita salad (hold cheese, request guacamole on the side and order salsa for dressing)

Mama's taco salad (request substitution of flour tortillas for shell and guacamole on the side, hold cheese, and order salsa for dressing)

Fresh tossed salad t dressing on side)

Grilled Chicken

Pollo a la parrilla, single breast

Pechuga monterrey, single breast (hold cheese)

Menu has helpful section that defines Mexican foods. Light ranch dressing available.

Fajitas (request vegetarian frijoles rancheros)

Beef or chicken (1/2 pound)

Combination (1/2 pound)

Chimichangas and Burritos (request rice and vegetarian frijoles rancheros)

Sonora style burrito (hold sour cream and cheese)

Roasted brisket burrito (hold sour cream and cheese)

A la Carte

Frijoles rancheros (vegetarian)

Rice

Pico de Gallo

Single tamale

Single enchilada

Bean chalupa

Enchilada dinners (request rice and vegetarian frijoles rancheros)

Seasoned ground beef (2)

Chicken (2) (hold sour cream)

PUTTING IT ALL TOGETHER

Light Choice

(Low in calories, fat, and cholesterol)

Mama's taco salad with ground beef (hold guacamole and tortilla shell)

Tortilla (2)

Pico de Gallo (4 tbsp., use for dressing)

Nutrition Values:

Calories	539
Carbohydrate (gm.)	47
Protein (gm.)	32
Fat (gm.)	26
% calories from fat	43
Cholesterol (mg.)	81
Sodium (mg.)	1189

Exchanges:. 3 Starch/Breads, 3 Meats (medium), 2 Vegetables, 2 Fats

Moderate Choice

(Moderate in calories, low in fat and cholesterol)

Single enchilada, chicken (request light on cheese)

Enchilada sauce (2 oz., extra on side)

Refried beans (2/3 cup)

Pico de gallo (2 oz.)

White wine*(6 oz.)

Nutrition Values:

Calories	761
Carbohydrate (gm.)	77
Protein (gm.)	42
Fat (gm.)	17
% calories from fat	20
Cholesterol (mg.)	79
Sodium (mg.)	1510

Exchanges: 4 Starch/Breads, 3 Meats (medium), 2 Vegetables , 2 Fats

Alcohol not accounted for in exchanges

ORIGINAL EL TORITO'S

Best Bets

Antojitos (Appetizers)
Chunky chicken quesadilla (hold the cheese and share or order as entree)
Sopa Y Ensaladas (Soups and Salads)
Fajitas taco salad, steak or chicken (hold shell, cheese, and sour cream, request whole wheat tortillas and extra pico de gallo)
Garden Salad (dressing on side or request salsa for dressing)
Tortilla soup (hold cheese)
Combinaciones (Combinations)
Enchiladas (2) (hold corn cake and add garden salad)
Enchilada/chile relleno (hold corn cake, add garden salad)

Especialidades (Specialties)
Arroz con pollo (hold cheese sauce and sour cream, request served with whole wheat tortillas)
Grilled soft tacos, chicken or steak (request made with whole wheat tortillas and extra salsa, hold corn cake and guacamole)
Sizzling fajitas (suggest share entree, request whole wheat tortillas and extra salsa, hold sour cream)
Steak, Chicken, Shrimp
Burritos
Burrito especial (request whole wheat tortilla, hold cheese)
Seafood burrito (request whole wheat tortilla, hold sour cream and cheese)
A la Carta
Enchilada, beef or chicken
Chile relleno
Tortillas, corn, flour, or whole wheat
Mexican-style rice

El Torito's uses only 100 percent cholesterol-free vegetable oil and light sour cream.

PUTTING IT ALL TOGETHER

Light Choice
(Low in calories, fat, and cholesterol)
Garden salad with salsa dressing
Chicken enchilada (a la carta, light on cheese)
Mexican rice (a la carta)

Nutrition Values:
Calories 707
Carbohydrate (gm.) 79
Protein (gm.) 39
Fat (gm.) 26
% calories from fat 33
Cholesterol (mg.) 87
Sodium (mg.) 2200*
*High in sodium

Exchanges: 4 Starch/Breads, 3 Meats (lean), 3 Vegetables, 3 Fats

Moderate Choice
(Moderate in calories, low in fat and cholesterol)
Tortilla soup (hold cheese)
Shrimp fajitas (share order) (request six whole-wheat tortillas and extra salsa)
Refried beans (share order) (1/3 cup)
Beer* (light) 12 oz.

Nutrition Values:
Calories 866
Carbohydrate (gm.) 107
Protein (gm.) .41
Fat (gm.) 23
% calories from fat 24
Cholesterol (mg.) 153
Sodium (mg.) 1342

Exchanges: 6 Starch/Breads, 3 Meats (lean), 2 Vegetables, 3 Fats
*Alcohol not accounted for in exchanges

TACO BELL

Best Bets

	Calories	Carbohydrate (gm.)	Protein (gm.)	Fat (gm.)	Cholesterol (mg.)	Sodium (mg.)
Soft taco	265	29	12	12	32	554
Tostada with red sauce	243	27	9	11	16	596
Chicken soft taco	259	31	14	10	52	681
Steak fajita	279	27	15	12	39	653
Chicken fajita	276	25	17	11	52	689
Bean burrito	458	83	15	14	9	1231
Beef burrito	508	68	25	21	57	1394
Burrito Supreme®	517	75	20	22	33	1264
Chicken burrito	411	58	17	12	52	963
Combo burrito	484	66	18	16	33	1219
Chilito	460	56	18	18	47	893
Cinnamon Twists	171	24	2	8	0	234
Taco sauce (1 tbsp.)	2	0	0	0	0	126
Hot taco sauce (1 tbsp.)	3	0	0	0	0	82
Salsa (1 tbsp.)	18	4	1	0	0	376
Pico de gallo (2 tbsp.)	6	1	0	0	1	66
Red sauce (2 tbsp.)	10	2	0	0	0	261
Green sauce (2 tbsp.)	4	1	0	0	0	136

No lard, tropical oil, MSG, or sulfites are used. The chain uses skinless, oven-roasted chicken.

PUTTING IT ALL TOGETHER

Light Choice
(Low in calories, fat, and cholesterol)
Bean burrito, Pico de gallo

Nutrition Values:
Calories 464
Carbohydrate (gm.) 84
Protein (gm.) .15
Fat (gm.) 14
% calories from fat 27
Cholesterol (mg.) 9
Sodium (mg.) 1297

Exchanges: 5 Starch/Breads,
2 Vegetables, 3 Fats

Moderate Choice
(Moderate in calories, low in fat and cholesterol)
Tostada, Chicken soft taco, Pico de
gallo, Cinnamon Twist, Milk (2%) 8 oz.

Nutrition Values:
Calories 799
Carbohydrate (gm.) 95
Protein (gm.) .33
Fat (gm.) 34
% calories from fat 38
Cholesterol (mg.) 83
Sodium (mg.) 1697

Exchanges: 5 Starch/Breads, 2 Meats
(medium), 2 Vegetables, 5 Fats

TACO JOHN'S

Best Bets

	Calories	Carbohydrate (gm.)	Protein (gm.)	Fat (gm.)	Cholesterol (mg.)	Sodium (mg.)
Softshell taco with chicken	180	20	18	8	n/a	490
Taco Bravo® (hold sour cream)	319	42	16	14	n/a	658
Bean burrito (hold sour cream)	197	37	12	6	n/a	636
Chicken burrito (hold sour cream and cheese)	227	19	27	10	n/a	639
Super burrito, hold sour cream and cheese	389	51	18	16	n/a	856
Super burrito with chicken, hold sour cream and cheese	366	40	30	14	n/a	844
Smothered burrito with green chili, hold sour cream and cheese	367	40	20	18	n/a	998
Taco salad without dressing, hold sour cream, cheese, and shell	228	30	13	13	n/a	440
Super taco salad without dressing, hold sour cream, cheese, and shell	428	59	21	20	n/a	900
Chicken super taco salad without dressing, hold sour cream and cheese	377	56	26	15	n/a	882
Mexican rice	340	59	7	8	n/a	1280

Nutrition information provided by Taco John's is based on usual preparation. If an item is eaten without cheese, sour cream, or tortilla shell, nutrient information will change accordingly.

n/a = no cholesterol information provided.

PUTTING IT ALL TOGETHER

Light Choice
(Low in calories, fat, and cholesterol)
Chicken super taco salad (hold shell
  and sour cream, request extra
  hot sauce)
Mexican rice (share the order)

Nutrition Values*:
Calories	547
Carbohydrate (gm.)	86
Protein (gm.)	30
Fat (gm.)	19
% calories from fat	31
Cholesterol (mg.)	n/a
Sodium (mg.)	1522

Exchanges:
5 Starch/Breads, 2 Meats (lean),
2 Vegetables, 3 Fats

Moderate Choice
(Moderate in calories, low in fat and cholesterol)
Super burrito with chicken
  (hold sour cream)
Taco Bravo® (hold sour cream)

Nutrition Values:
Calories	685
Carbohydrate (gm.)	82
Protein (gm.)	46
Fat (gm.)	22
% calories from fat	29
Cholesterol (mg.	n/a
Sodium (mg.)	1502

Exchanges:
5 Starch/Breads, 4 Meats (medium),
2 Vegetables

*Nutrition values based on data obtained from Taco John's. With special requests as noted,
fat and calories will be less.*

TACO TIME

Best Bets

	Calories	Carbohydrate (gm.)	Protein (gm.)	Fat (gm.)	Cholesterol (mg.)	Sodium (mg.)
Chicken taco salad without dressing	436	35	31	19	70	521
Chicken taco salad without dressing and cheese	381	33	29	15	56	436
Veggie salad without dressing and cheese	302	36	12	13	0	715
Side salad without dressing and cheese	51	5	3	3	0	11
Mexican brown rice	160	28	2	2	0	540
Refritos without cheese	293	38	11	11	0	834
Chicken soft taco	390	34	31	12	70	322
Chicken soft taco without cheese	335	32	29	8	56	237
Veggie burrito	535	71	21	20	20	890
Veggie burrito without sour cream	502	71	21	17	14	883
Veggie burrito without sour cream and cheese	477	69	18	13	0	798
Soft flour taco without cheese	331	34	19	12	26	599
Soft combo burrito	550	55	30	24	48	1227
Soft combo burrito without cheese	462	65	17	14	0	1095
Soft bean burrito	547	68	22	21	20	1027
Soft bean burrito without cheese	462	65	17	14	0	895
Soft meat burrito without cheese	467	40	32	19	53	1295
Tostada delight® meat without sour cream and cheese	410	42	22	17	25	916

TACO TIME (cont.)

	Calories	Carbohydrates (gm.)	Protein (gm.)	Fat (gm.)	Cholesterol (mg.)	Sodium (mg.)
Taco cheese burger without dressing and cheese	397	49	20	13	17	1071
Taco salad with out dressing	347	22	23	16	35	720
Casita burrito® without sour cream and cheese	427	46	23	17	25	1243
Enchilada sauce (1 oz.)	14	3	0	0	0	115
Hot sauce (1 oz.)	10	2	0	0	0	120
Ranchero sauce (2 oz.)	18	3	1	1	0	115
Casa sauce (1 oz.)	40	10	0	0	0	180
Mexican dressing, nonfat (2 oz.)	20	5	0	0	0	130

Taco Time offers brochures with nutrition information with and without dressings and cheese. No lard is used in cooking beans and chicken is skinless, white breast meat. Fat-free Mexican dressing is available.

PUTTING IT ALL TOGETHER

Light Choice
(Low in calories, fat, and cholesterol)
Soft meat burrito (hold cheese)
Side salad (hold cheese and dressing)
Enchilada sauce (4 tbsp.)

Nutrition Values:
Calories 546
Carbohydrate (gm.) 51
Protein (gm.) .35
Fat (gm.) 22
% calories from fat 35
Cholesterol (mg.) 53
Sodium (mg.) 1536

Exchanges:
3 Starch/Breads, 3 Meats (medium),
2 Vegetables, 1 Fat

Moderate Choice
(Moderate in calories, low in fat and cholesterol)
Veggie burrito (hold sour cream)
Mexican brown rice
Side salad (hold dressing and cheese)
Ranchero sauce (4 tbsp.)

Nutrition Values:
Calories 731
Carbohydrate (gm.) 107
Protein (gm.) .27
Fat (gm.) 23
% calories from fat 28
Cholesterol (mg. 14
Sodium (mg.) 1549

Exchanges:
6 Starch/Breads, 3 Vegetables, 4 Fats

PIZZA AND MORE

In the realm of quick and easy food choices, pizza is undeniably healthy. It's basically flour, tomato sauce, and cheese, sometimes even part-skim cheese. Nutritionally, pizza beats a burger and fries by a long shot. In a basic thin crust cheese pizza, the calories range between 150 to 200 calories a slice (depending on whether it's from a large pie), with a bit of fat and cholesterol from cheese, and a few hundred milligrams of sodium.

The nutrition profile for a basic piece of cheese pizza is very different from that of deep-dish with pepperoni, sausage, and extra cheese. The calories and fat also creep in when the thin crust becomes thicker or deeper. Unfortunately, a trend in the pizza chain industry seems to be "25% more toppings" and "more cheese". This may increase sales, but it also increases waistlines.

Beyond hiding pizza's health virtues under sausage, hamburger, and extra cheese, the biggest nutritional downfall of pizza eating is overeating. The old commercial said it best: "Bet you can't eat just one," or even two. The secret to keeping pizza healthy is keep it simple or load on the veggies, count the slices, and fill up on crunchable greens.

Nutrition Pros

■ Pizza matches today's nutrition goals: low fat, moderate protein, and heavy on the carbohydrates.
■ Design your own pizza with the healthiest and healthier toppings. (See Best Bets)
■ Healthier pizza is easily made to order; compliment it with a side salad or trip to the salad bar.
■ Most chains offer one veggie combination pizza.
■ If you're counting calories, stick with the thin crust pizza and load on the veggies.
■ Salads or salad bars often compliment the pizza. (See page 6 for salad bar information.)
■ More and more chains are providing nutrition facts, allowing you to pick and choose knowledgeably.

Nutrition Cons

■ Healthy pizza can quickly become unhealthy with extra cheese, pepperoni, Italian sausage.
■ Some chains tout "extra cheese" and "more toppings." That doesn't promote good health.
■ Restaurant-designed combinations load on the unhealthy toppings.
■ Healthy sounding bread—sticks or garlic—are often doused in fat and cheese.
■ "Vegetarian" is not necessarily a healthy descriptor. Cheese may be layered, shredded, or melted.

BERTUCCI'S

Best Bets

Appetizers/Salads
Insalata—full and half portions
Soup/Chowder:
Tuscan minestrone soup
Pasta
Gnocchi (hold or light on cheese)
Linguine with clam sauce
Linguine with prosciutto, spinach, and
  mushrooms (substitute tomato sauce)
Rigatoni
Rigatoni alla Bertucci (substitute
  tomato sauce)
Rigatoni, broccoli, and chicken
  (substitute light white wine sauce)

*Tomato sauce can be substituted for cream
sauce in any pasta dish.*

Specialty Pizza
Romano
Quattro stagioni
Marengo
Melanzana
Clam pizza
Create your own pizza
Toppings—Healthiest
  Broccoli florets
  Crushed garlic
  Green peppers
  Hot cherry peppers
  Spinach
  Tomato slices
  White mushrooms
  White onions
Toppings—Healthier
  Artichoke hearts
  Black olives
  Caramelized onions
  Eggplant
  Roasted peppers

PUTTING IT ALL TOGETHER

Light Choice
(Low in calories, fat, and cholesterol)
Clam pizza (2 slices, small)
Insalata—half portion (hold cheese)
  with 2 tbsp. house Italian dressing
  on the side

Nutrition Values:
Calories 475
Carbohydrate (gm.) 45
Protein (gm.) .30
Fat (gm.) 21
% calories from fat 40
Cholesterol (mg.) 33
Sodium (mg.) 1211

Exchanges: 3 Starch/Breads, 3 Meats
(medium), 1 Fat

Moderate Choice
(Moderate in calories, low in fat and cholesterol):
Rigatoni, broccoli, and chicken (request
  tomato sauce instead of cream sauce)
Tuscan minestrone soup (hold Romano
  cheese)
Wine, white (6 oz.)*

Nutrition Values:
Calories 859
Carbohydrate (gm.) 90
Protein (gm.) .46
Fat (gm.) 23
% calories from fat 24
Cholesterol (mg.) 154
Sodium (mg.) . . . . .2490†
                              † High in sodium.
Exchanges: 5 Starch/Breads, 4 Meats
(lean), 1 Vegetable, 2 Fats
    †Alcohol not accounted for in exchanges.

CALIFORNIA PIZZA KITCHENS

Best Bets

Soup & Salad (always have dressing on side)
Canadian bay shrimp (add to any salad)
Chopped salad (hold salami and cheese, request Canadian bay shrimp instead)
Field greens salad
Greek style salad
Oriental chicken salad
Sedona white corn tortilla soup
Shrimp Louie (substitute balsamic basil vinaigrette for Louie dressing)

Pizza (about the size of a dinner plate, available with honey wheat crust)

Carribean shrimp
Fresh tomato
Grilled eggplant cheeseless
Grilled teriyaki chicken
Mixed grill vegetarian
Original BBQ chicken
Roasted garlic chicken
Rosemary chicken-potato
Southwestern burrito (hold sour cream)
Tandoori chicken
Thai chicken
Traditional cheese
Vegetarian

Calzone
Moo shu chicken calzone
Buffalo mozzarella calzone

Pasta
Bolognese
Broccoli/sun-dried tomato
Ginger black bean sauce
Italian salsa
Marsala-marinara with chicken or shrimp
Mediterranean
Primavera
Thai chicken
Tomato-basil
Tomato-herb

Grilled Items
Grilled breast of chicken

Pizza Buns (order with spicy Szechuan slaw)
Chicken
Grilled rosemary chicken

Cheeseless Pizza
Grilled eggplant
Thai
Vegetarian

Desserts
Haagen-Dazs frozen low-fat yogurt
Sorbets

Several cheeseless pizzas are listed on menu. In addition, any pizza can be prepared without cheese. This chain does not use any MSG.

PUTTING IT ALL TOGETHER

Light Choice
(Low in calories, fat, and cholesterol)
Mediterranean pasta with angel
  hair or penne spaghetti
Mixed leaf salad, half portion
  (hold cheese) with 2 tbsp. balsamic
  basil vinaigrette on side

Nutrition Values:
Calories 487
Carbohydrate (gm.) 59
Protein (gm.) 10
Fat (gm.) 22
% calories from fat 41
Cholesterol (mg. 0
Sodium (mg.) 1365

Exchanges:
3 Starch/Breads, 2 Vegetables, 4 Fats

Moderate Choice
(Moderate in calories, low in fat and cholesterol)
Field greens salad (half portion) with
  2 tbsp. balsamic dijon on side
Thai chicken pizza (2 slices)
Fruit sorbet (share)

Nutrition Values:
Calories 701
Carbohydrate (gm.) 74
Protein (gm.) 36
Fat (gm.) 30
% calories from fat 39
Cholesterol (mg. 62
Sodium (mg.) 1294

Exchanges: 3 Starch/Breads, 3 Meats
(medium), 2 Vegetables, 1 Fruit, 3 Fats

FUN FOOD FACTS

• Tradition has it that the Polo brothers, Niccolo and Maffeo, and
Niccolo's son Marco, returned from China around the end of the 13th
century with recipes for the preparation of Chinese noodles. It is
known with greater certainty that the consumption of pasta in the
form of spaghetti-like noodles and turnip-shaped ravioli was firmly
established in Italy by 1353. *Extraordinary Origins of Everyday Things,
1987.*

• The largest pizza ever baked measured 122 feet, 8 inches in diameter,
made at Norwood Hypermarket, Norwood, South Africa, on December 8, 1990. *Guiness Book of Records, 1992.*

CHUCK E. CHEESE'S SHOWBIZ PIZZA PLACE

Best Bets

Pizza
Cheese (small, medium, large)
Combination pizza
Vegetarian pizza

Toppings—Healthiest
Green peppers
Jalapeno
Mushrooms
Onions
Tomatoes

Toppings—Healthier
Black olives
Canadian bacon

Salad bar (handle with care)

Italian breadsticks

PUTTING IT ALL TOGETHER

Light Choice
(Low in calories, fat, and cholesterol)
Cheese pizza, medium, 2 slices
  with jalapenos and black olives
Salad bar with 2 tbsp. Italian dressing
  and vinegar. (See page 6 for salad
  bar information.

Nutrition Values:
Calories 650
Carbohydrate (gm.) 69
Protein (gm.) .29
Fat (gm.) 30
% calories from fat 42
Cholesterol (mg.) 26
Sodium (mg.) 1821

Exchanges:
3 Starch/Breads, 3 Meats (medium),
2 Vegetables, 3 Fats

Moderate Choice
(Moderate in calories, low in fat and cholesterol)
Cheese pizza, medium, 3 slices with
  pineapple, ham, and onions
Beer, light (12 oz.)*

Nutrition Values:
Calories 711
Carbohydrate (gm.) 70
Protein (gm.) .47
Fat (gm.) 19
% calories from fat 24
Cholesterol (mg.) 30
Sodium (mg.) 1642

Exchanges:
4 Starch/Breads, 4 Meats (medium),
2 Vegetables
  †*Alcohol not accounted for in exchanges.*

DOMINO'S PIZZA

Best Bets

	Calories	Carbohydrate (gm.)	Protein (gm.)	Fat (mg.)	Cholesterol (mg.)	Sodium (mg.)
Pizza						
12-inch Veggie pizza, 1 slice	204	27	12	5	9	488
12-inch Pepperoni pizza, 1 slice	219	30	9	7	14	570

Combination pizza
Vegi Pizza Feast™
Cheese pizza (medium, large)

Onion
Pineapple

Toppings—Healthiest
Green pepper
Mushroom

Toppings—Healthier
Black olive
Ham

PUTTING IT ALL TOGETHER

Light Choice
(Low in calories, fat, and cholesterol)

Vegi Pizza Feast™, 12-inch pizza,
2 slices

Nutrition Values:
Calories 409
Carbohydrate (gm.) 55
Protein (gm.) 23
Fat (gm.) 11
% calories from fat 24
Cholesterol (mg.) 18
Sodium (mg.) 976

Exchanges:
3 Starch/Breads, 3 Meats (lean),
2 Vegetables

Moderate Choice
(Moderate in calories, low in fat and cholesterol)

Pepperoni pizza, medium, 12-inch,
3 slices

Nutrition Values:
Calories 656
Carbohydrate (gm.) 89
Protein (gm.) 26
Fat (gm.) 22
% calories from fat 30
Cholesterol (mg.) 42
Sodium (mg.) 1710

Exchanges:
5 Starch/Breads, 1 Meats (lean),
2 Vegetables, 3 Fats

GODFATHER'S

Best Bets

Pizza
Cheese—Original or Golden Crust
(small, medium, large)
Vegetarian combo

Salad
Salad bar (handle with care)
Salad to go

Fresh breadsticks with sauce

Toppings—Healthiest
Green peppers
Jalapeno
Mushrooms
Onions
Pineapple

Toppings—Healthier
Black olives
Green olives
Ham

	Calories	Carbohydrates (gm.)	Protein (gm.)	Fat (mg.)	Cholesterol (mg.)	Sodium (mg.)
Original Crust—Cheese Pizza						
Mini (1/4)	138	20	6	4	13	159
Small (1/6)	239	32	10	7	25	289
Medium (1/8)	242	35	10	7	22	285
Large (1/10)	271	37	12	8	28	329
Golden Crust - Cheese Pizza						
Small (1/6)	213	27	8	8	19	258
Medium (1/8)	229	28	8	9	19	272
Large (1/10)	261	31	8	11	23	314

PUTTING IT ALL TOGETHER

Light Choice
(Low in calories, fat, and cholesterol)
2 fresh breadsticks with marinara sauce
Salad bar with 2 tbsp. French dressing
and vinegar. (See page 6 for salad
bar information.
Nutrition Values:
Calories 604
Carbohydrate (gm.) 82
Protein (gm.) .16
Fat (gm.) 27
% calories from fat 41
Cholesterol (mg.) 4
Sodium (mg.) 1916

Exchanges: 5 Starch/Breads,
3 Vegetables, 4 Fats

Moderate Choice
(Moderate in calories, low in fat and cholesterol)
Original crust mini cheese pizza
(1 whole)
Beer, light (12 oz.)*

Nutrition Values:
Calories 651
Carbohydrate (gm.) 85
Protein (gm.) .25
Fat 16
% calories from fat 22
Cholesterol (mg.) 52
Sodium (mg.) 1167

Exchanges: 5 Starch/Breads, 2 Meats
(medium), 1 Vegetable, 1 Fat
* Alcohol not accounted for in exchanges.

LITTLE CAESARS PIZZA

Best Bets

Pizza
Cheese (small, medium, large)*

Toppings—Healthiest
Extra sauce
Green pepper

Hot pepper rings
Jalapeno
Mushroom
Onion
Pineapple

Toppings—Healthier
Black olive
Canadian bacon
Ham

	Calories	Carbohydrate (gm.)	Protein (gm.)	Fat (gm.)	Cholesterol (mg.)	Sodium (mg.)
Pizza!Pizza!®: Cheese Pizza—Round						
Small	138	14	9	5	15	200
Medium	154	16	10	5	15	220
Large	169	18	11	6	15	240
Cheese Pizza—Square						
Small	188	22	10	6	20	380
Medium	185	22	10	6	20	370
Large	188	22	10	6	20	380
Individual Orders						
Baby Pan!Pan!®	525	53	28	22	60	1180
Crazy Bread® (one piece)	98	18	4	1	2	119
Crazy Sauce®	63	11	3	1	0	360
Salads & Sandwiches						
Greek salad (small)*	85	6	4	5	10	400
Ham & cheese† **	553	47	32	27	50	1580
Tossed salad (small)*	37	7	2	1	0	85
Turkey sandwich†	450	49	24	17	45	1590

Medium size also available; no nutrition information available.
†*High in sodium.*
**Hold cheese.*
Mozzarella is made from part skim milk.

PUTTING IT ALL TOGETHER

Light Choice
Low in calories, fat, and cholesterol
Baby Pan!Pan!® (cheese)

Nutrition Values:
Calories 525
Carbohydrate (gm.) 53
Protein (gm.) 28
Fat (gm.) 22
% calories from fat 38
Cholesterol (mg.) 60
Sodium (mg.) 1180

Exchanges: 3 Starch/Breads
2 Meats (medium), 2 Vegetables, 2 Fats

Moderate Choice
Moderate in calories, low in fat and cholesterol
Greek salad, medium, with 2 tbsp. Italian salad dressing
Crazy bread® (4 sticks)
Crazy sauce ® (1 serving)

Nutrition Values:
Calories 762
Carbohydrate (gm.) 98
Protein (gm.) .27
Fat (gm.) 29
% calories from fat 34
Cholesterol (mg. 28
Sodium (mg.) 1868

Exchanges: 5 Starch/Breads, 1 Meat (medium), 3 Vegetables, 5 Fats

FUN FOOD FACTS

• Market share by pizza type in 1990: Thin 53%, Thick 23%, Stuffed 2%, Pan 22%; compared with 1987, Thin 59%, Thick 25%, Stuffed 2%, Pan 14%. *Restaurant Hospitality, December, 1991.*

MAZZIO'S PIZZA

Best Bets

Pizza
Cheese (mini, small, medium, large)*

Toppings—Healthiest
Green peppers
Jalapeno
Mushrooms
Onions
Pineapple

Toppings—Healthier
Black olives
Canadian bacon
Green olives
Ham

Salad
Chef salad
Salad bar (choose with care)

Entree
Baked lasagna
Chicken Parmesan
Spaghetti

	Calories	Carbohydrate (gm.)	Protein (gm.)	Fat (gm.)	Cholesterol (mg.)	Sodium (mg.)
Deep pan cheese	350	42	17	13	15	620
Original crust cheese*	260	33	14	8	10	450
Thin crust cheese	220	22	13	9	15	440
Chicken Parmesan† **	590	68	39	19	50	1600
Spaghetti, small	290	39	11	10	5	800

* Based on 2 slices of medium pizza.
† Served with salad and garlic bread (hold garlic bread). Nutrition information does not include salad or toasted garlic bread.
•• High in sodium.

Cheese used is part skim milk, and low-calorie salad dressing available.

PUTTING IT ALL TOGETHER

Light Choice
(Low in calories, fat, and cholesterol)

Deep pan pizza, cheese, 1 slice
Salad bar with 2 tbsp. ranch dressing
and vinegar (See page 6 for salad bar
information.)

Nutrition Values:
Calories.	.637
Carbohydrate (gm.)	78
Protein (gm.)	26
Fat (gm.)	.28
% calories from fat	39
Cholesterol (mg.)	15
Sodium (mg.)	1370

Exchanges:
4 Starch/Breads, 1 Meat (medium),
3 Vegetables, 4 Fats

Moderate Choice
(Moderate in calories, low in fat and cholesterol)

Chicken Parmesan (hold garlic bread)
with pasta and marinara sauce
Salad with 2 tbsp. Italian dressing and
vinegar

Nutrition Values:
Calories	752
Carbohydrate (gm.)	.78
Protein (gm.)	.41
Fat (gm.)	.34
% calories from fat	.40
Cholesterol (mg.)	50
Sodium (mg.)	1832

Exchanges:
4 Starch/Breads, 4 Meats (lean),
2 Vegetables, 4 Fats

MR. GATTI'S

Best Bets

Pizza
Cheese with topping(s)—choose
 from healthy toppings
Combination pizza
Original crust pizza, cheese
 (small, medium, large)
Vegetarian Sampler®

Toppings—Healthiest
Fresh bell peppers
Fresh mushrooms
Fresh onions
Fresh diced tomatoes

Toppings—Healthier
Black olives
Canadian bacon
Green olives
Jalapeno

Salad
Gatti's garden salad

Entree
SpaGatti® Jr. (hold garlic bread)

PUTTING IT ALL TOGETHER

Light Choice
(Low in calories, fat, and cholesterol)
SpaGatti® Jr. (hold garlic bread)
Salad with 2 tbsp. ranch dressing
 and vinegar
Wine, white (6 oz.)*

Nutrition Values:
Calories 666
Carbohydrate (gm.) 52
Protein (gm.) .22
Fat (gm.) 30
% calories from fat 41
Cholesterol (mg.) 75
Sodium (mg.) 1731

Exchanges:
3 Starch/Breads, 2 Meats (medium),
1 Vegetable, 4 Fats
 * Alcohol not accounted for in exchanges.

Moderate Choice
(Moderate in calories, low in fat, cholesterol)
Vegetarian Sampler® (4 pieces)

Nutrition Values:
Calories 684
Carbohydrate (gm.) 77
Protein (gm.) .42
Fat (gm.) 24
% calories from fat 31
Cholesterol (mg.) 52
Sodium (mg.) 1847

Exchanges:
4 Starch/Breads, 4 Meats (medium),
2 Vegetables, 1 Fat

PAPA GINO'S

Pizza
Papa's Famous Pizza (small, large, thick pan)
Cheese with topping(s)—choose from healthy toppings
Combination: Super Veggie

Toppings—Healthiest
Mushrooms
Onions
Peppers

Toppings—Healthier
Black olives

Festa di Pasta!: (tomato/meat sauce)
Fettucini
Spaghetti or ziti
Tortellini
Subs/Pockets, Small (Request plenty of lettuce, tomatoes, onions, pickles, hot peppers; hold oil or mayonnaise)
Hot ham and cheese
Meatball
Turkey breast
Vegetarian Pocket (light on the cheese)
Salad
All-you-can-eat salad bar (choose from the raw vegetables, use low-calorie dressing)
One-trip salad bar
Salad in a pocket
Desserts
Columbo® frozen non-fat yogurt, small without blend-ins

PUTTING IT ALL TOGETHER

Light Choice
(Low in calories, fat, and cholesterol)
Vegetarian Pocket (light on cheese, hold oil and mayonnaise, load on lettuce, tomatoes, pickles and hot peppers)
Frozen yogurt (6 oz.)

Nutrition Values:
Calories 427
Carbohydrate (gm.) 54
Protein (gm.) 15
Fat (gm.) 17
% calories from fat 36
Cholesterol (mg.) 22
Sodium (mg.) 1041

Exchanges: 2 Starch/Breads, 1 Meat (medium), 2 Vegetables, 1 Fruit, 2 Fats

Moderate Choice
(Moderate in calories, low in fat and cholesterol)
Cheese pizza, medium, 2 slices with onions and peppers
Salad bar with 2 tbsp. Italian dressing and vinegar. (See page 6 for salad bar information.)

Nutrition Values:
Calories 655
Carbohydrate (gm.) 79
Protein (gm.) 30
Fat (gm.) 28
% calories from fat 38
Cholesterol (mg.) 26
Sodium (mg.) 1347

Exchanges: 4 Starch/Breads, 2 Meats (medium), 3 Vegetables, 3 Fats

PETER PIPER PIZZA

Best Bets

Pizza
Original—small (10"), medium (12"),
 large (14"), extra large (16")
Mucho—small (10"), medium (12"),
 large (14"), extra large (16")

Toppings—Healthiest
Fresh green peppers
Jalapeno

Fresh mushrooms
Fresh onions
Pineapple
Fresh sliced tomatoes

Toppings—Healthier
Black olives
Ham

Salad
Chef salad
Garden salad
Side salad

	Calories	Carbohydrates (gm.)	Protein (gm.)	Fat (gm.)	Cholesterol (mg.)	Sodium (mg.)
Original pizza, small^						
Cheese (no topping)	163	15	16	4	8	227
Cheese with one topping						
Black olive	171	15	16	6	8	276
Green pepper	163	15	16	4	8	283
Ham	172	15	17	5	11	317
Jalapeno	163	15	16	4	8	283
Mushroom	162	15	16	4	8	245
Onion	162	15	16	4	8	228
Pineapple	164	15	16	4	8	228
Original pizza, medium^						
Cheese (no topping)	181	16	18	5	9	255
Cheese with one topping						
Black olive	193	17	18	6	9	303
Green pepper	183	17	18	5	9	256
Ham	194	16	19	6	13	356
Jalapeno	183	17	18	5	9	319
Mushroom	183	17	18	5	9	283
Onion	183	17	18	5	9	257
Pineapple	185	17	18	5	8	256

	Calories	Carbohydrates (gm.)	Protein (gm.)	Fat (gm.)	Cholesterol (mg.)	Sodium (mg.)
Original pizza, large*						
Cheese (no topping)	242	22	23	7	12	339
Cheese with one topping						
Black olive	259	22	24	8	12	407
Green pepper	245	22	24	7	12	339
Ham	258	22	26	7	17	473
Jalapeno	244	22	24	7	12	424
Mushroom	245	22	24	7	12	379
Onion	243	22	24	7	12	341
Pineapple	246	23	23	7	12	341

Information provided per slice.

PUTTING IT ALL TOGETHER

Light Choice
(Low in calories, fat, and cholesterol)
Cheese pizza, medium, 2 slices with jalapenos
Garden salad with 2 tbsp. French dressing and vinegar

Nutrition Values:
Calories 458
Carbohydrate (gm.) 43
Protein (gm.) .37
Fat (gm.) 17
% calories from fat 33
Cholesterol (mg.) 19
Sodium (mg.) 862

Exchanges:
2 Starch/Breads, 4 Meats (medium), 2 Vegetables

Moderate Choice
(Moderate in calories, low in fat and cholesterol)
Cheese pizza, medium, 3 slices with mushrooms
Garden salad with 2 tbsp. Italian dressing and vinegar

Nutrition Values:
Calories 711
Carbohydrate (gm.) 60
Protein (gm.) .54
Fat (gm.) 29
% calories from fat 37
Cholesterol (mg.) 26
Sodium (mg.) .1089

Exchanges:
3 Starch/Breads, 5 Meats (medium), 2 Vegetables

PIZZA HUT

Best Bets

Pizza
Pan, Thin 'n Crispy®, hand-tossed
traditional cheese with topping(s)—
choose from healthy toppings
Combination: Veggie Lover's®

Toppings—Healthiest
Green peppers
Jalapeno
Mushrooms
Onions

Toppings—Healthier
Black olives
Ham

Salad
Salad bar (choose with care)—as a meal
or with a meal

Entrees Pasta—spaghetti with meat sauce
Sandwiches—Meatball Supreme (hold cheese)

	Calories	Carbohydrate (gm.)	Protein (gm.)	Fat (gm.)	Cholesterol (mg.)	Sodium (mg.)
Hand-tossed, cheese pizza	259	28	17	10	28	638
Pan pizza, cheese	246	29	15	9	17	470
Thin 'n Crispy®, cheese	199	19	14	9	17	434

Nutrition information based on 1 slice of medium pizza. Pizza Hut® information provided per 2 slices medium.

PUTTING IT ALL TOGETHER

Light Choice
(Low in calories, fat, and cholesterol)
Thin 'n Crispy® pizza, medium, 2 slices
with: Ham, Jalapenos, Peppers
Milk, 2% (8 oz.)

Nutrition Values:
Calories 635
Carbohydrate (gm.) 52
Protein (gm.) 51
Fat (gm.) 26
% calories from fat 37
Cholesterol (mg.) 88
Sodium (mg.) 2080*
* Ham is high in sodium

Exchanges: 2 Starch/Breads, 4 Meats
(medium), 2 Vegetables, 1 Milk (2%)

Moderate Choice
(Moderate in calories, low in fat and cholesterol)
Pan pizza, 2 slices medium cheese
Salad bar with 2 tbsp. Thousand
Island dressing and vinegar.
(See page 6 for salad bar information.)
Beer, light (12 oz.)†

Nutrition Values:
Calories 888
Carbohydrate (gm.) 101
Protein (gm.) 40
Fat (gm.) 32
% calories from fat 33
Cholesterol (mg. 44
Sodium (mg.) 1728

Exchanges: 5 Starch/Breads, 3 Meats
(medium), 3 Vegetables, 3 Fats
† Alcohol not accounted for in exchanges.

PIZZERIA UNO

Appetizers
Chicken thumbs (with salad for
  entree)
*Veggie dip

Salad
Grilled chicken (light on cheese,
  hold bacon, dressing on the side)
House salad (oil and vinegar,
  hold cheese and croutons)
Spinach salad (hold bacon,
  dressing on side)

Plizzettas (thin crust pizza)
BBQ chicken
BBQ shrimp
*Cheeseless
Eggplant and artichoke
Seasame chicken
Simply cheese

Chicago Original Deep Dish Pizza
Spinoccoli
Veggie

*Several menu items are "formulated for lower
fat and cholesterol content." They are marked
here with asterisk (*).*

PUTTING IT ALL TOGETHER

Light Choice
(Low in calories, fat, and cholesterol)
House salad (hold cheese) with 2 tbsp.
  house vinaigrette dressing on side
Spinoccoli pizza, small (split or take
  half home)

Nutrition Values:
Calories 705
Carbohydrate (gm.) 78
Protein (gm.) 36
Fat (gm.) 32
% calories from fat 41
Cholesterol (mg.) 34
Sodium (mg.) 1636

Exchanges: 4 Starch/Breads, 3 Meats
(medium), 3 Vegetables, 2 Fats

Moderate Choice
(Moderate in calories, low in fat and cholesterol)
Cheeseless plizzetta, 2 slices
Spinach salad with 2 tbsp. house
  vinaigrette dressing on side (hold
  bacon)
Wine, white (6 oz.)*

Nutrition Values:
Calories 877
Carbohydrate (gm.). 96
Protein (gm.) 25
Fat (gm.) 34
% calories from fat 35
Cholesterol (mg.) 94
Sodium (mg.) 1716

Exchanges: 5 Starch/Breads,
3 Vegetables, 5 Fats
  * Alcohol not accounted for in exchanges.

ROUND TABLE PIZZA

Best Bets

Pizza
Personal, small, medium, large,
  ex-large
Cheese with topping(s)—choose
  from healthy toppings
Combination: Vegetarian

Toppings—Healthiest
Extra sauce
Green peppers
Jalapeno
Mushrooms

Onions
Pineapple
Shrimp
Tomatoes
Toppings—Healthier
Ham
Olives
Salad Bar:
All you can eat
Single serving
Salad (prepackaged)
Family serving
Single serving
Sandwiches
Ham (hold cheese and mayonnaise)
Pastrami (hold cheese and mayo)
Turkey (hold cheese and mayonnaise)

	Calories	Carbohydrate (gm.)	Protein (gm.)	Fat (gm.)	Cholesterol (mg.)	Sodium (mg.)
Pizza, thin cheese	166	18	8	7	21	332
Pizza, pan cheese	310	40	13	11	30	631

Nutrition information based on 1 slice large pizza.

PUTTING IT ALL TOGETHER

Light Choice
(Low in calories, fat, and cholesterol)
Thin cheese pizza, 3 slices (large)
  with extra sauce, onions, peppers,
  and shrimp

Nutrition Values:
Calories 651
Carbohydrate (gm.) 70
Protein (gm.) .37
Fat (gm.) 25
% calories from fat 35
Cholesterol (mg.) 150
Sodium (mg.) 1392

Exchanges: 4 Starch/Breads
3 Meats (medium), 2 Vegetables, 2 Fats

Moderate Choice
(Moderate in calories, low in fat and cholesterol)
Turkey sandwich on French roll
  (hold cheese)
Single serving salad with 2 tbsp. Thou-
  sand Island dressing and vinegar
Apple juice (12 oz.)

Nutrition Values:
Calories 665
Carbohydrate (gm.) 84
Protein (gm.) 42
Fat (gm.) 18
% calories from fat 24
Cholesterol (mg.) 104
Sodium (mg.) 1251

Exchanges: 3 Starch/Breads, 4 Meats
(medium), 1 Vegetable, 2 Fruits, 1 Fat

SHAKEY'S

Best Bets

Pizza

Cheese with topping(s)—choose from
  healthy toppings
Combination: Vegetarian, Pesto
  chicken
Individual, small, medium, large
Toppings—Healthiest
Green onions
Green peppers
Jalapeno
Onions
Red bell peppers
Sun-dried tomatoes
White mushrooms
Toppings—Healthier
Black olives
Canadian bacon
Pasta
Pasta marinara (split portion)
Spaghetti with meat sauce
  (split portion)
Salads
Family size salad
Garden salad
Sandwiches
Pesto chicken (hold cheese)
Smoked ham and cheese (hold cheese)

	Calories	Carbohydrate (gm.)	Protein (gm.)	Fat (gm.)	Cholesterol (mg.)	Sodium (mg.)
Thin crust						
Cheese	133	13	8	5	14	323
Thin crust—toppings: Onions, green peppers, black olives, mushrooms	125	14	7	5	11	313
Thick crust						
Cheese	170	22	9	5	13	421
Thick crust with: Onions, green peppers, black olives, mushrooms	162	22	9	4	13	418
Homestyle crust						
Cheese	303	31	14	14	21	591
Homestyle crust with: Onions, green peppers, black olives, mushrooms	320	32	15	15	21	652
Spaghetti with meat sauce	940	134	26	33	n/a	1904†
Hot ham and cheese and garlic bread*	550	56	36	21	n/a	2135†

Nutrition information based on 1 slice (1/10) of a 12" pizza.
* Hold garlic bread or split serving.   † High in sodium.

PUTTING IT ALL TOGETHER

Light Choice
(Low in calories, fat, and cholesterol)
Fresh garden salad with 2 tbsp. oil and vinegar
Pesto chicken sandwich on sourdough roll (hold cheese)

Nutrition Values:
Calories 561
Carbohydrate (gm.) 40
Protein (gm.) .42
Fat (gm.) 27
% calories from fat 43
Cholesterol (mg.) 96
Sodium (mg.) 1378

Exchanges:
2 Starch/Breads, 4 Meats (medium),
2 Vegetables, 3 Fats

Moderate Choice
(Moderate in calories, low in fat and cholesterol)
(Split both items)
Spaghetti and meat sauce (served with garlic bread)*
Thin crust pizza, 2 slices (from 12" pizza, with onion, green pepper, black olives, mushroom)

Nutrition Values:
Calorie 720
Carbohydrate (gm.) 95
Protein (gm.) 27
Fat (gm.) 26
% calories from fat 33
Cholesterol (mg.) . . . . n/a
Sodium (mg.) 1578

Exchanges:
5 Starch/Breads, 2 Meats (medium),
3 Vegetables, 3 Fats

* *Nutrition information includes garlic bread; excluding garlic bread would decrease nutrition values.*

SANDWICH AND SUB CHAINS

It's called a hoagie, hero, grinder, sub, submarine, and wedge. But whatever its name, it's a long sandwich usually loaded with Italian meats, vegetables, and spicy toppers.

Although Italian meats are the traditional sandwich topping, sub chains now stuff sandwiches with sauteed vegetables, cheese, turkey, roast beef, ham, tuna, and seafood salad. Many restaurants also offer sandwiches on a variety of fresh-baked breads, plus salads and soups.

The main nutrition pitfall to sandwiches and subs is not the bread, as many people think—it's the meat. For instance, a 12-inch cold cut combo packs enough protein for the whole day. And common sandwich ingredients such as cheese, oil, and mayonnaise, just add calories and fat.

The good news is that these ingredients are easily avoided because sandwiches are generally made while you wait. Encourage your sandwich creator to hold the cheese, oil, and mayonnaise, and go light on the meat. The heavy hand can be used when applying the lettuce, tomatoes, onions, pickles, and hot peppers. Complement sandwiches with a salad, cup of broth-based soup, popcorn, or pretzels

Nutrition Pros

■ Healthy breads, even some with extra fiber, are found, such as pita pockets, whole grain rolls, honey wheat subs.
■ Go for the unadulterated fillers: turkey, flame-broiled chicken, roast beef, or ham.
■ Pack on the pickles and peppers for low-calorie zip.
■ Mustard and vinegar add taste and moistness without calories.
■ Smaller portions are being added as lower cost menu items.
■ Salads are an option for the main course or side.
■ Frozen yogurt is becoming a regular offering.

Nutrition Cons

■ Like most American food, subs and sandwiches are heavy on the protein and fat, light on the carbohydrates.
■ Sandwich additions—mayonnaise and oil—are high in fat.
■ Cheese is everywhere—layered on sandwiches, melted on vegetables, or sprinkled on meatballs.
■ Low-calorie salad dressings are often extremely high in sodium.

AU BON PAIN

Best Bets for Breakfast

Fresh Rolls	Calories	Carbohydrate (gm.)	Protein (gm.)	Fat (gm.)	Cholesterol (mg.)	Sodium (mg.)
Petit pain	220	44	7	<1	0	490
Hearth	250	45	10	2	0	510
Alpine	220	43	8	3	0	810
Vegetable	230	40	6	5	0	410
Rye	230	44	8	2	0	n/a
Pumpernickel	210	42	8	2	0	1005
Country seed	220	37	9	4	0	460
3 Seed raisin	250	46	8	4	0	480
Gourmet Muffins						
Bran	390	73	7	11	20	940
Blueberry	390	66	8	4	40	410
Cranberry walnut	350	53	7	13	15	730
Oat bran apple	400	71	7	2	0	590
Bagels (all)	270	n/a	n/a	1	n/a	n/a

Fresh squeezed orange juice (no information provided)
Apple juice (no information provided)

PUTTING IT ALL TOGETHER

Light Choice for Breakfast
(Low in calories, fat, and cholesterol)
Hearth roll and Preserves (1 pkg)
Apple juice (10 oz.)

Nutrition Values:
Calories 423
Carbohydrate (gm.) 88
Protein (gm.) 10
Fat (gm.) 2
% calories from fat 4
Cholesterol (mg.) 0
Sodium (mg.) 520

Exchanges:
3 Starch/Breads, 3 Fruits

Moderate Choice for Breakfast
(Moderate in calories, low in fat, cholesterol)
Onion bagel and Cream cheese
Orange juice (10 oz.)

Nutrition Values:
Calories 511
Carbohydrate (gm.) 85
Protein (gm.) 14
Fat (gm.) 12
% calories from fat 21
Cholesterol (mg.) 31
Sodium (mg.) 361

Exchanges:
3 Starch/Breads, 3 Fruits, 2 Fats

Best Bets for Lunch or Dinner

	Calories	Carbohydrate (gm.)	Protein (gm.)	Fat (gm.)	Cholesterol (mg.)	Sodium (mg.)
Fresh Salads						
Large garden	40	8	3	<1	0	20
Small garden	20	5	5	<1	0	10
Chicken tarragon garden	310	11	24	15	70	332
Grilled chicken garden	110	9	14	2	30	330
Cracked pepper chicken garden	100	9	14	2	25	360
Shrimp garden	102	8	11	2	105	193
Low-calorie Italian	68	3	0	6	5	360
Hot Soups						
Split pea, cup	176	30	12	1	<1	303
bowl	264	45	18	2	1	453
Minestrone, cup	105	20	5	2	1	265
Beef barley, cup	75	10	6	2	12	600
bowl	112	15	9	3	18	901
Sandwich Rolls*						
French sandwich	320	65	10	<1	0	710
Hearth sandwich	370	69	16	3	0	600
Soft roll	310	50	8	8	0	410
Sandwich Fillings* (based on one serving for a full sandwich)						
Country ham	150	3	17	7	115	970
Smoked turkey	100	0	22	1	35	950
Roast beef	180	1	24	8	60	310
Chicken tarragon	270	3	24	15	70	304
Cracked pepper chicken	120	1	23	2	50	680
Grilled chicken	130	1	23	4	60	610

Sandwiches can be made with any bread or roll and any filling.

Cookies

Oatmeal raisin	250	41	4	9	10	230

AU BON PAIN (cont.)

PUTTING IT ALL TOGETHER

Light Choice for Lunch or Dinner
(Low in calories, fat, and cholesterol)
Minestrone soup, cup
Half sandwich, cracked pepper chicken
   on French roll
Apple (medium)

Nutrition Values:
Calories 490
Carbohydrate (gm.) 73
Protein (gm.) 25
Fat (gm.) 6
% calories from fat 11
Cholesterol (mg.) 61
Sodium (mg.) 1391

Exchanges:
4 Starch/Breads, 2 Meats (lean), 1 Fruit

Moderate Choice for Lunch or Dinner
(Moderate in calories, low in fat, cholesterol)
Sandwich, smoked turkey with
   mustard on hearth sandwich roll
Oatmeal raisin cookie (1)

Nutrition Values:
Calories 720
Carbohydrate (gm.) 110
Protein (gm.) 42
Fat (gm.) 19
% calories from fat 24
Cholesterol (mg.) 45
Sodium (mg.) 1780

Exchanges:
5 Starch/Breads, 4 Meats (lean), 2
Fruits, 1 Fat

BLIMPIE

Best Bets

Subs, cold* (3-inch quik bite
   or 6-inch regular)
Roast beef
Turkey
Ham & Swiss (hold cheese if desired)

Subs, hot* (3-inch quik bite
   or 6-inch regular)
Roast beef American (hold cheese
   if desired)
Meatball

Salads
Chef salad
Tossed salad

Lites, salad or pita sandwich
   (all under 300 calories)
Roast beef
Ham & Swiss (hold cheese if desired)
Seafood and crab

Extras
Hot or sweet peppers
Pickle, spear/whole (high in sodium)

*Served on wheat, white, or pita bread. All sandwiches dressed with tomatoes, lettuce, onions, and special sauce. Request plenty of tomatoes, lettuce, and onions. Hold special sauce, mayonnaise, and oil. Use mustard if desired.

PUTTING IT ALL TOGETHER

Light Choice
(Low in calories, fat, and cholesterol)
Seafood and crab pita sandwich from
    lite menu (hold extra mayonnaise,
    add plenty of lettuce, tomatoes,
    onions, pickles, and hot peppers)
Popcorn (1 small bag)

Moderate Choice
(Moderate in calories, low in fat, cholesterol)
Ham and cheese sub
    (6 inch or half regular)
Pretzels (1 small bag)
Tossed salad with oil (2 tsp.) and
    vinegar (2 tbsp.)

Nutrition Values:

Calories	.478
Carbohydrate (gm.)	.52
Protein (gm.)	.18
Fat (gm.)	.23
% calories from fat	.43
Cholesterol (mg.)	.28
Sodium (mg.)	1678

Nutrition Values:

Calories	539
Carbohydrate (gm.)	71
Protein (gm.)	23
Fat (gm.)	15
% calories from fat	.25
Cholesterol (mg.)	37
Sodium (mg.)	1322

Exchanges:
3 Starch/Breads, 2 Meats (lean),
1 Vegetable, 3 Fats

Exchanges:
4 Starch/Breads, 2 Meats (medium),
2 Vegetables, 1 Fat

D'ANGELO

Best Bets

	Calories	Carbohydrate (gm.)	Protein (gm.)	Fat (gm.)	Cholesterol (mg.)	Sodium (mg.)
Pita Pokkets and Submarines*						
Steak d'lite pokket	415	n/a	n/a	11	91	500
Roast beef d'lite pokket	325	n/a	n/a	5	63	730
Roast beef d'lite small sub	365	n/a	n/a	7	63	750
Meatball (sub only)	(no nutrition information)					
Turkey d'lite pokket	350	n/a	n/a	4	64	500
Turkey d'lite small sub	390	n/a	n/a	6	64	520
Stir fry chicken d'lite pokket	340	n/a	n/a	4	60	1025
Vegetarian d'lite pokket	350	n/a	n/a	11	26	995

*Order pita pokket or small sub for individual serving; medium or large sub for sharing. Order with plenty of lettuce, sliced tomatoes, onions, pickles, hot peppers, mustard, or ketchup. Hold oil and mayonnaise.

D'ANGELO (cont.)	Calories	Carbohydrate (gm.)	Protein (gm.)	Fat (gm.)	Cholesterol (mg.)	Sodium (mg.)
Super Salads*, served with Syrian pocket bread						
Tuna salad d'lite	305	n/a	n/a	2	32	805
Turkey salad d'lite	375	n/a	n/a	4	64	660
Roast beef salad d'lite	350	n/a	n/a	5	63	890
Chicken salad d'lite	325	n/a	n/a	4	49	980
Frozen Yogurt						
Low-fat frozen yogurt (5 oz.)	130	n/a	n/a	3	31	55
Low-fat frozen yogurt (5 oz.) in waffle cone	220	n/a	n/a	3	31	60

*Low-calorie dressings served on side: lite Italian, fat-free raspberry vinaigrette, or cranberry vinaigrette.

D'Angelo provides a nutrition brochure called "The Choice is Yours." Nutrition information is also included in their menu.

PUTTING IT ALL TOGETHER

Light Choice
(Low in calories, fat, and cholesterol)
Roast beef super salad d'lite
   with fat-free raspberry vinaigrette
Low-fat frozen yogurt (5 oz.)

Nutrition Values:
Calories 480
Carbohydrate (gm.) 55
Protein (gm.) 34
Fat (gm.) 12
% calories from fat 17
Cholesterol (mg.) 94
Sodium (mg.) 945

Exchanges:
3 Starch/Breads, 2 Meats (lean), 2 Vegetables

Moderate Choice
(Moderate in calories, low in fat, cholesterol)
Steak and mushroom pokket d'lite
Low-fat frozen yogurt (5 oz.)
   in waffle cone

Nutrition Values:
Calories 635
Carbohydrate (gm.) 79
Protein (gm.) 46
Fat (gm.) 15
% calories from fat 21
Cholesterol (mg.) 123
Sodium (mg.) 680

Exchanges:
5 Starch/Breads, 4 Meats (lean), 1 Fat

MIAMI SUBS

Best Bets

Subs, cold* (junior size available)
Vegetarian cheese sub
Turkey breast (hold Mayonnaise)

Subs, hot*
Roast beef (hold Mayonnaise)
Meatball Parmesan
Ham and cheese (hold cheese if
desired; hold mayonnaise)

Chicken†
Flame-broiled chicken breast (plain
or with mushrooms)

Burgers
Super burger (flame-broiled 5-oz.
burger on Kaiser roll. Request plenty
of lettuce, tomatoes, and onions.
Hold mayonnaise)

Pita Specialties
Gyro on pita bread
Flame-broiled chicken breast on pita
Cheese vegetarian on pita

Fresh Salads (light Italian dressing
available)
Garden salad
Greek salad
Chef's salad
Broiled chicken club salad
Sliced turkey breast salad

Nonfat Frozen Yogurt (small or large

*All subs include Swiss American cheese (hold if desired). Request plenty of lettuce, tomatoes,
onions. Hold "secret sauce," and mayonnaise and oil, if added,
† Served on Kaiser roll. Request plenty of tomatoes and lettuce. Hold mayonnaise.

PUTTING IT ALL TOGETHER

Light Choice
(Low in calories, fat, and cholesterol)
Greek salad with light Italian
dressing on side (4 tbsp.)
Pita bread (plain, not grilled)
Milk (2%), 8 oz.
Pear (from home)

Nutrition Values:
Calories 538
Carbohydrate (gm.) 73
Protein (gm.) 23
Fat (gm.) 19
% calories from fat 32
Cholesterol (mg.) 68
Sodium 2182**
**High in sodium*

Exchanges:
3 Starch/Breads, 2 Meats (medium),
2 Vegetables, 1 Fat

Moderate Choice
(Moderate in calories, low in fat, cholesterol)
Vegetarian cheese sub, regular (hold
oil, add plenty of lettuce, tomatoes,
onions, pickles, and hot peppers)
Non-fat frozen yogurt (small—5 oz.)

Nutrition Values:
Calories 665
Carbohydrate (gm.) 96
Protein (gm.) 23
Fat (gm.) 20
% calories from fat 27
Cholesterol (mg.) 50
Sodium (mg.) 1130

Exchanges:
5 Starch/Breads, 1 Meat (medium),
2 Vegetables, 3 Fats

SCHLOTZSKY'S

Best Bets

Original Sandwiches*
Smoked turkey original (light version; hold mayonnaise, use mustard)

Light Sandwiches*
Smoked turkey breast
(hold mayonnaise)
Chicken breast
Dijon turkey breast
The Vegetarian (hold ranch dressing)

Hot Deli Sandwiches*
Roast beef and cheddar (hold cheese and mayonnaise, request mustard)

Schlotzsky's uses light mayonnaise.
*Choose from fresh-baked sourdough, wheat, or dark rye breads.

Specialty Sandwiches*
Texas Schlotzsky's (hold cheese and mayonnaise, request mustard)

Sourdough Crust Pizza
Chicken and pesto
Vegetarian special
Barbecue chicken
Grilled onion and mushrooms
Smoked turkey and peppers

Salads (light Italian dressing available)
Smoked turkey chef salad
Chicken chef salad
Chef's salad
Tossed salad

Soup
Daily flavor, only if broth-based
(vegetable, chicken noodle, etc.)

PUTTING IT ALL TOGETHER

Light Choice
(Low in calories, fat, and cholesterol)
Dijon turkey breast on whole wheat
roll (request plenty of lettuce and
tomatoes)
Cup of soup
(broth- or vegetable-based)

Nutrition Values:
Calories 623
Carbohydrate (gm.) 67
Protein (gm.) 51
Fat (gm.) 16
% calories from fat 23
Cholesterol (mg.) 97
Sodium (mg.) . . . . 2034†
†High in sodium

Exchanges:
4 Starch/Breads, 4 Meats (lean),
1 Vegetable, 1 Fat

Moderate Choice
(Moderate in calories, low in fat, cholesterol)
Vegetarian special, sourdough
crust pizza (2 slices)
Tossed salad with light Italian
dressing (3 tbsp.)

Nutrition Values:
Calories 659
Carbohydrate (gm.) 65
Protein (gm.) 30
Fat (gm.) 33
% calories from fat 45
Cholesterol (mg.) 53
Sodium (mg.) . . . . 2840†
†High in sodium

Exchanges:
3 Starch/Breads, 2 Meats (medium),
3 Vegetables, 4 Fats

SUBWAY

Best Bets

	Calories	Carbohydrate (gm.)	Protein (gm.)	Fat (gm.)	Cholesterol (mg.)	Sodium (mg.)
Sandwiches*						
Cold cut combo, Italian, 12 inch	853	83	46	40	166	2218
Cold cut combo, honey wheat, 12 inch	882	88	48	41	166	2278
Subway club, Italian, 12 inch	693	83	46	22	84	2716
Subway club, honey wheat, 12 inch	722	89	47	23	84	2776
Meatball, Italian, 12 inch	917	96	42	44	88	2022
Meatball, honey wheat, 12 inch	947	101	44	45	88	2082
Steak and cheese, Italian, 12 inch	765	83	43	32	82	1556
Steak and cheese, honey wheat, 12 inch	711	89	41	33	82	1615
Roast turkey breast, white, 6 inch	312	n/a	n/a	8	31	1119
Turkey breast, Italian, 12 inch	645	83	40	19	67	2459
Turkey breast, honey wheat, 12 inch	674	88	42	20	67	2520
Roast beef, Italian, 12 inch	689	84	42	23	75	2287
Roast beef, honey wheat, 12 inch	717	89	41	24	75	2347
Ham and cheese, Italian, 12 inch	643	81	38	18	73	1709
Ham and cheese, honey wheat, 12 inch	673	86	39	22	73	2508
Veggies and cheese, honey wheat, 6 inch	258	n/a	n/a	6	10	530
Veggies and cheese, Italian, 12 inch	535	81	20	17	19	1076

Suggestion: divide 12-inch sandwich into two meals. Request plenty of lettuce, tomatoes, pickles, bell peppers. Hold oil and mayonnaise, and cheese if desired. Use mustard as a substitute.

SUBWAY (cont.)
Salads**

	Calories	Carbohydrate (gm.)	Protein (gm.)	Fat (gm.)	Cholesterol (mg.)	Sodium (mg.)
Cold cut combo, small	305	12	18	25	83	908
Subway club, small	224	12	18	13	42	989
Turkey breast, small	201	12	15	11	33	861
Roast beef, small	222	13	16	10	38	775
Ham & cheese, small	200	11	14	12	36	855
Lite Italian dressing (4 tbsp.)	23	4	trace	1	trace	952

**Salad dressing not included in nutrition information.*

Subway provides nutrition information in a booklet. Nutrient content reflects how foods are usually prepared. Special requests will change nutrition information. Fresh-baked honey wheat or Italian bread is used.

PUTTING IT ALL TOGETHER

Light Choice
(Low in calories, fat, and cholesterol)
Roast beef submarine on honey wheat, 12 inch (have half wrapped or share; hold oil, mayonnaise, add plenty of lettuce, tomatoes, onions, pickles, and peppers)
Cheese popcorn (1 small bag)

Nutrition Values:
Calories 508
Carbohydrate (gm.) 59
Protein (gm.) 24
Fat (gm.) 21
% calories from fat 37
Cholesterol (mg.) 38
Sodium (mg.) 1359

Exchanges:
4 Starch/Breads, 2 Meats (lean), 2 Fats

Moderate Choice
(Moderate in calories, low in fat, cholesterol)
Meatball submarine on honey wheat, 12 inch (share sandwich, hold oil, add plenty of lettuce, tomatoes, onions)
Veggie cheese salad, reg. (hold cheese) with 4 tbsp. lite Italian dressing

Nutrition Values:
Calories 685
Carbohydrate (gm.) 66
Protein (gm.) 22
Fat (gm.) 31
% calories from fat 41
Cholesterol (mg.) 63
Sodium (mg.) 2329*
High in sodium

Exchanges:
4 Starch/Breads, 2 Meats (medium), 2 Vegetables, 4 Fats

SEAFOOD

Broiled cod, blackened salmon, or steamed Alaskan crab claws conjure up "good for you" notions. Seafood restaurants have diligently ridden the coat tails of the loudly chanted health message, "eat more fish." When prepared with little fat, (an important caveat), fish is low in saturated fat, has minimal cholesterol, is complete protein, and is light in calories.

Unfortunately, the nutritional virtues of seafood are lost in most chain restaurants, especially the fast food types. As fish is battered, fried and surrounded by French fries, covered with Alfredo sauce, or floated in garlic butter, the once healthy seafood is now part of a fat-and calorie-dense meal.

On the other hand, table-service restaurants do offer healthy options. Broiled, blackened, or grilled fish are regulars. Shrimp cocktail or steamed shellfish are also standards. Entrees are available with a selection of healthy sides, from baked potato to rice, salads and/or vegetables.

With seafood's health qualities in mind, you'd think dining in seafood chains would be a snap. Sadly, that's far from the truth. Read the fine print and get ready to dodge the fats. Creative ordering, special requests, and perhaps the hardest of all, portion control, can turn any seafood restaurant meal into a healthy delight.

Nutrition Pros

■ A la carte ordering can be your saving grace.
■ In fast food restaurants, portions are relatively small and nothing greets you at the table.
■ Some chains offer bottomless salads. But remember, a good thing can be overdone, expecially if overdressed.
■ In table-service restaurants, grilled, blackened, steamed, and baked are common cooking techniques.
■ Low-calorie salad dressings and low-fat cocktail sauce are usually offered.
■ Lemon is cut and ready to squirt.

Nutrition Cons

■ Fried is the name of the game from entrees to sides.
■ Menu descriptors are deceiving in fast food chains. When in doubt, assume fried.
■ Beware high-fat tartar sauce and other mayonnaise-based fat.
■ The sodium can be very high.

ARTHUR TREACHER'S

Best Bets

Entrees
Broiled fish dinner (1 piece fish, roll,
   baked potato, coleslaw)
A la Carte Items
Broiled fish (1 piece)
Baked potato
Milk (2%)

*Arthur Treacher's uses 100% cholesterol-
free oil (peanut). Baked potato may be
substituted wherever chips are offered.*

FUN FOOD FACTS

• **Delmonico's (the famous New
York restaurant) put Lobster
Newburg on the menu as Lobster
a la Wenberg. After a quarrel between Wenberg and Delmonico,
the name was changed to
Newberg by reversing the letters
of the first syllable.** *A History of
Food and Drink in America, 1981*

PUTTING IT ALL TOGETHER

Light Choice
(Low in calories, fat, and cholesterol)
Order a la Carte
Broiled fish (1 piece)
Baked potato with margarine (1 pat)
Coleslaw (1 cup)

Nutrition Values:
Calories	475
Carbohydrate (gm.)	61
Protein (gm.)	25
Fat (gm.)	15
% calories from fat	29
Cholesterol (mg.)	75
Sodium (mg.)	1407

Exchanges:
3 Starch/Breads, 2 Meats (lean),
1 Vegetable, 2 Fats

Moderate Choice
(Moderate in calories, low in fat, cholesterol)
Broiled fish dinner (1 piece fish, roll,
   baked potato, coleslaw)
Milk (2%), 8 oz.

Nutrition Values:
Calories	709
Carbohydrate (gm.)	90
Protein (gm.)	36
Fat (gm.)	22
% calories from fat	28
Cholesterol (mg.)	93
Sodium (mg.)	1800

Exchanges:
4 Starch/Breads, 2 Meats (lean),
2 Vegetables, 1 Milk (2%), 2 Fats

CAPTAIN D'S

Best Bets

	Calories	Carbohydrate (gm.)	Protein (gm.)	Fat (gm.)	Cholesterol (mg.)	Sodium (mg.)
Broiled and Baked Dinners						
Orange roughy dinner*	537	56	35	19	39	2156
Shrimp dinner*	457	34	56	10	191	2194
Chicken dinner*	414	55	30	8	71	2615
Baked fish dinner†	659	62	36	30	54	1767
Green beans (seasoned)	46	5	2	2	4	752
White beans	126	22	8	1	2	99
Rice	124	28	3	0	0	9
Breadstick (1)	91	17	3	1	0	210
Dinner salad (no dressing)	27	3	1	1	1	67
Italian dressing— low calorie (2 tbsp.)	9	2	0	0	0	568
Crackers (4)	50	8	1	1	3	147
Cocktail sauce (2 tbsp.)	34	8	0	0	0	252
Sweet & sour sauce (2 tbsp.)	52	13	0	0	0	5

Green beans, rice, side salad, corn-on-the-cob may be substituted for French fries or coleslaw.
* *Calculated with rice, green beans, breadstick, and salad.*
† *Calculated with rice, green beans, breadstick, and coleslaw.*

PUTTING IT ALL TOGETHER

Light Choice
(*Low in calories, fat, and cholesterol*)
Baked orange roughy dinner (rice, green beans, salad, and breadstick)
Ranch dressing (2 tbsp.)

Nutrition Values:
Calories 631
Carbohydrate (gm.) 56
Protein (gm.) 35
Fat (gm.) 29
% calories from fat 41
Cholesterol (mg.) 54
Sodium (mg.) .... 2386+
+High in sodium
Exchanges: 3 Starch/Breads, 3 Meats (lean), 2 Vegetables, 4 Fats

CAPTAIN D'S (cont.)

PUTTING IT ALL TOGETHER

Moderate Choice
(Moderate in calories, low in fat, cholesterol)
Broiled fish dinner (rice, green beans, coleslaw, and breadstick)

Nutrition Values:

Calories 659
Carbohydrate (gm.) 62
Protein (gm.) 36
Fat (gm.) 30
% calories from fat 41
Cholesterol (mg.) 54
Sodium (mg.) 1767

Exchanges: 3 Starch/Breads, 3 Meats (lean), 3 Vegetables, 4 Fats

L & N SEAFOOD

Best Bets

Appetizers
Creole gumbo
Shrimp cocktail

Seafood Pasta (hold garlic cheese toast)
Linguini with red clam sauce
Linguini with shrimp marinara
Linguini and white clam sauce

Dinner Salad and Sandwiches
L & N's seafood salad grill
Soup and caesar combination (choose creole gumbo and request house salad instead of caesar)
Blackened chicken salad (dressing on side)
Blackened fish sandwich (substitute baked potato or cup of gumbo or house salad for French fries)
Texas chicken salad (substitute baked potato or cup of gumbo or house salad for French fries)
Blackened fish sandwich
Texas chicken sandwich

Combination Platters (share)
Broiled seafood platter
Combination grill

Today's Fresh Catch
Any fish—broiled, baked, or steamed (with house salad, red skin potatoes, and vegetable)
Fresh lobster—steamed, no butter, served with lemon wedges

Shrimp
Barbecued shrimp skewer
Grilled shrimp skewer

Shellfish
Grilled shrimp and scallop skewer
Broiled sea scallops
Alaskan snow crab legs

Beef and Poultry (share)
Grilled marinated chicken (hold onion straws)
Grilled Texas chicken (hold onion straws)
Filet mignon (hold onion straws)

Express Lunch
Linguini and red clam sauce
Blackened chicken salad
Linguini with white clam sauce
Grilled herbed chicken

Combinations
Seafood salad grill (house or spinach salad and fresh fish or grilled shrimp skewer)
Soup and salad (house or spinach salad with spicy creole gumbo)

PUTTING IT ALL TOGETHER

Light Choice
(Low in calories, fat, and cholesterol)
Salad with olive oil (2 tsp.) and vinegar (2 tbsp.)
Linguini and shrimp marinara (hold garlic cheese toast)

Nutrition Values:
Calories 633
Carbohydrate (gm.) 76
Protein (gm.) 36
Fat (gm.) 24
% calories from fat 34
Cholesterol (mg.) 175
Sodium (mg.) 2025*
High in sodium

Exchanges:
4 Starch/Breads, 3 Meats (lean),
3 Vegetables, 2 Fats

Moderate Choice
(Moderate in calories, low in fat, cholesterol)
Shrimp cocktail (share)
Salad with French dressing (2 tbsp.) on side
Broiled seafood platter (share)
Rice pilaf
Vegetables
Beer, light (12 oz.) †

Nutrition Values:
Calories 842
Carbohydrate (gm.) 71
Protein (gm.) 61
Fat (gm.) 27
% calories from fat 29
Cholesterol (mg.) 270**
Sodium (mg.) 2571**
**High in cholesterol (shrimp) and sodium*

Exchanges:
3 Starch/Breads, 6 Meats (lean),
3 Vegetables, 2 Fats
†Alcohol not accounted for in exchanges

FUN FOOD FACTS

• Until the end of the 19th century, lobster was so plentiful it was used for fish bait. Alas, with ever-increasing popularity, those days are gone. The most popular variety in the U.S. is the Maine lobster. *Food Lover's Companion, 1990*

LONG JOHN SILVER'S

Best Bets

	Calories	Carbohydrate (gm.)	Protein (gm.)	Fat (gm.)	Cholesterol (mg.)	Sodium (mg.)
Baked Entrees						
Baked fish with lemon crumbs (3 pieces)*	610	86	39	13	125	1420
Light portion fish with lemon crumbs (2 pieces)†	330	46	24	5	75	640
Chicken*	590	82	32	15	75	1620
Salads						
Ocean chef salad**	110	13	12	1	40	730
Small salad**	25	6	1	<1	0	20
A La Carte Items						
Baked fish with lemon crumbs (3 pieces—5 oz.)	150	4	29	1	110	370
Chicken—light herb	120	<1	22	4	60	570
Seafood chowder with cod	140	10	11	6	20	590
Green beans	20	3	1	<1	3	320
Rice	160	30	3	3	0	340
Small salad	25	6	1	<1	0	20
Roll	110	23	4	<1	0	170
Saltine crackers (2)	25	4	<1	1	0	75
Oatmeal raisin cookie	160	15	3	10	15	150
Condiments						
Seafood sauce (1 tbsp.)	14	3	<1	<1	0	180
Honey mustard sauce (1 tbsp.)	20	5	<1	<1	0	60
Sweet n' sour	20	5	<1	<1	0	45

* *Calculated including rice, green beans, coleslaw, and a roll (no margarine).*
† *Calculated including rice and small salad, without dressing.*
** *Calculated without salad dressing or crackers.*

PUTTING IT ALL TOGETHER

Light Choice
(Low in calories, fat, and cholesterol)
Seafood chowder (7 oz.)
Ocean chef salad
Saltines (6)
Seafood sauce (2 tbsp.)

Nutrition Values:
Calories 353
Carbohydrate (gm.) 41
Protein (gm.) 26
Fat (gm.) 12
% calories from fat 31
Cholesterol (mg.) 60
Sodium (mg.) 1905

Exchanges:
2 Starch/Breads, 2 Meats (lean)
2 Vegetables, 1 Fat

Moderate Choice
(Moderate in calories, low in fat, cholesterol)
Fish with lemon crumbs (3 pieces) with
    rice, green beans, coleslaw, and roll
Oatmeal raisin cookie (1)

Nutrition Values:
Calories 770
Carbohydrate (gm.) 101
Protein (gm.) 42
Fat (gm.) 23
% calories from fat 27
Cholesterol (mg.) 140
Sodium (mg.) 1570

Exchanges:
6 Starch/Breads, 3 Meats (lean)
2 Vegetables, 3 Fats

RED LOBSTER

Best Bets

Appetizers	Calories	Carbohydrate (gm.)	Protein (gm.)	Fat (gm.)	Cholesterol (mg.)	Sodium (mg.)
Shrimp cocktail (6 large)	90	n/a	n/a	2	175	80
Chilled shrimp in the shell (6 oz.)	130	n/a	n/a	2	250	120
Bayou-style seafood gumbo (6-oz. cup)	180	n/a	n/a	5	38	800
Bayou-style seafood gumbo (12-oz. bowl)	350	n/a	n/a	9	75	1600

RED LOBSTER (cont.)

Entrees*	Calories	Carbohydrate (gm.)	Protein (gm.)	Fat (gm.)	Cholesterol (mg.)	Sodium (mg.)
Live Maine lobster	200	n/a	n/a	5	180	680
Alaskan snow crab legs	200	n/a	n/a	11	120	1360
Broiled rock lobster	250	n/a	n/a	5	210	790
Grilled chicken and shrimp	490	n/a	n/a	20	300	1830
Grilled chicken salad	120	n/a	n/a	5	300	1240
Grilled chicken breast						
4 oz. lunch	170	n/a	n/a	6	70	230
8 oz. dinner	340	n/a	n/a	12	140	460
Grilled shrimp skewers (20 oz. shrimp)	170	n/a	n/a	9	390	120
Broiled flounder fillets (5 oz.)	150	n/a	n/a	6	80	370

Today's Fresh Catch† (representative sampling; all 5-oz. portions)

	Calories	Carbohydrate (gm.)	Protein (gm.)	Fat (gm.)	Cholesterol (mg.)	Sodium (mg.)
Atlantic cod	150	n/a	n/a	6	81	340
Grouper	150	n/a	n/a	6	79	340
Haddock	160	n/a	n/a	6	98	450
Lemon sole	160	n/a	n/a	6	75	360
Walley pike	160	n/a	n/a	6	75	55
Mahimahi	160	n/a	n/a	6	103	125
Snapper	160	n/a	n/a	6	84	410
Red rock fish	140	n/a	n/a	6	96	370
Yellow lake perch	170	n/a	n/a	6	143	360

Sandwiches**

	Calories	Carbohydrate (gm.)	Protein (gm.)	Fat (gm.)	Cholesterol (mg.)	Sodium (mg.)
Broiled fish fillet	230	n/a	n/a	10	80	450
Grilled chicken	340	n/a	n/a	10	70	430

Accompaniments

	Calories	Carbohydrate (gm.)	Protein (gm.)	Fat (gm.)	Cholesterol (mg.)	Sodium (mg.)
Rice pilaf (4 oz.)	140	n/a	n/a	3	0	390
Baked potato	150	n/a	n/a	2	0	410
Fresh vegetables without buttersauce	25	n/a	n/a	0	0	20
Shrimp vinaigrette dressing (3 tbsp.)	170	n/a	n/a	17	35	610
Lite Italian dressing (2 tbsp.)	50	n/a	n/a	3	0	220

	Calories	Carbohydrate (gm.)	Protein (gm.)	Fat (gm.)	Cholesterol (mg.)	Sodium (mg.)
Desserts						
Ice cream	260	n/a	n/a	14	60	110
Sherbert	180	n/a	n/a	2	10	60
Condiments						
Shrimp cocktail sauce	30	n/a	n/a	0	n/a	380

Red Lobster provides nutrition guide of healthier items "To Your Health".
* Information provided is only for fish/shellfish/chicken portion of meal, does not include accompaniments.
† All Today's Fresh Catch lunch portions are 5 oz. raw weight plus 1 teaspoon buttersauce. Dinner portions are 10 oz. raw weight plus 2 teaspoons buttersauce.
** No soup, fries, or coleslaw included in calculations.

PUTTING IT ALL TOGETHER

Light Choice
(Low in calories, fat, and cholesterol)
Today's Fresh Catch (request doggie bag with order and take half home)
Rice pilaf
Vegetable (hold buttersauce)
Salad with 2 tbsp. shrimp vinaigrette dressing on side
Sherbert

Nutrition Values:
Calories 648
Carbohydrate (gm.) 77
Protein (gm.) 38
Fat (gm.) 22
% calories from fat 31
Cholesterol (mg.) 136
Sodium (mg.) 1021

Exchanges:
3 Starch/Breads, 4 Meats (lean)
2 Vegetables, 1 Fruit, 2 Fats

Moderate Choice
(Moderate in calories, low in fat, cholesterol)
Bayou-style seafood gumbo (1 cup)
Salad with 2 tbsp. lite Italian dressing
Live Maine lobster (hold butter, plenty of lemon)
Baked potato (hold butter or sour cream)
Wine—white (6 oz.)†

Nutrition Values:
Calories 859
Carbohydrate (gm.) 102
Protein (gm.) 58
Fat (gm.) 18
% calories from fat 19
Cholesterol (mg.) 218*
Sodium (mg.) 2123*
*High in cholesterol and sodium

Exchanges:
5 Starch/Breads, 5 Meats (lean)
2 Vegetables
†Alcohol not accounted for in exchanges

SKIPPER'S

Best Bets

Entree	Calories	Carbohydrate (gm.)	Protein (gm.)	Fat (gm.)	Cholesterol (mg.)	Sodium (mg.)
Baked fish (4.4 oz.)	147	0	30	3	85	475
Baked salmon (4.4 oz.)	270	1	39	11	70	504
Alder smoked salmon chowder (6 oz.)	166	14	13	7	n/a	73
Clam chowder (1 cup)	100	14	3	4	12	525
Small green salad	59	6	3	3	13	223
Shrimp & seafood salad	167	15	23	3	80	657

Accompaniments

	Calories	Carbohydrate (gm.)	Protein (gm.)	Fat (gm.)	Cholesterol (mg.)	Sodium (mg.)
Baked potato	145	32	4	0	0	6
Side salad	24	4	0	0	0	8
Barbecue sauce (1 tbsp.)	25	5	0	1	0	226
Cocktail sauce (1 tbsp.)	20	5	0	0	0	216
Milk, low-fat (12 oz.)	181	32	15	10	0	225

PUTTING IT ALL TOGETHER

Light Choice
(Low in calories, fat, and cholesterol)
Clam chowder (1 cup)
Shrimp and seafood salad with cocktail sauce (2 tbsp.)
Baked potato with margarine (1 pat)

Nutrition Values:
Calories 488
Carbohydrate (gm.) 71
Protein (gm.) 30
Fat (gm.) 11
% calories from fat 20
Cholesterol (mg.) 92
Sodium (mg.) 1667

Exchanges:
4 Starch/Breads, 2 Meats (lean)
2 Vegetables, 1 Fat

Moderate Choice
(Moderate in calories, low in fat, cholesterol)
Baked fish
Baked potato with margarine (1 pat)
Side salad with Thousand Island dressing (2 tbsp.)
Milk, 2% (12 oz.)

Nutrition Values:
Calories 693
Carbohydrate (gm.) 76
Protein (gm.) 49
Fat (gm.) 21
% calories from fat 27
Cholesterol (mg.) 91
Sodium (mg.) 1176

Exchanges:
3 Starch/Breads, 4 Meats (lean)
1 Vegetable, 1 1/2 Milk (2%), 1 Fat

STEAK HOUSES

Two types of steak houses dot America's roadsides. The order at the counter, take a tray, and head to the mammoth food bar is one variety. These establishments, such as Ponderosa's and Ryan's, tout their value and loads of food for the dollar. The other type of steak houses offers the luxury of sit-down service. Steak & Ale, The Chart House, and a new and growing chain, Outback Steakhouse, are examples.

All steak houses, of course, focus on steak. But they also offer healthier chicken and fish entrees. Although potatoes and rice are common entree accompaniments, it's the "mega" food bars at many steak houses that get the attention. Notice they're not called salad bars. These food bars commonly offer fresh raw vegetables, cooked vegetables, pasta and meat salads, fresh and canned fruit, puddings, frozen yogurt, breads, muffins, and sweet breads.

The good news is that with some creative ordering and careful maneuvering around the food bar, it's easy to be health and nutrition conscious in steak houses.

Unfortunately, it's also easy to overeat and consume too much protein and fat. A 16-ounce sirloin has enough protein for a family of four. Your challenge is to outsmart the restaurant and arrange the meal so protein is the side dish, and starch, vegetables, and salad are the main course.

Nutrition Pros

■ Several leaner cuts of beef are served—filet mignon, sirloin tips, sirloin, chopped sirloin.
■ Smaller entree servings are available. Stick with cuts less than 6 ounces uncooked, unless sharing. If size is not indicated, ask.
■ Order meat as you like it, but trim well before eating.
■ Try items such as kabobs or sirloin tips which have less meat.
■ Fresh raw vegetables are plentiful at the food bars.

Nutrition Cons

■ Items are often high in protein and fat, low in carbohydrates.
■ High fat is still standard—high-fat cuts of meat, large portions, butter, sour cream, mayonnaise, and salad dressings.
■ Fried foods are prevalent, from French fried items to fried chicken, fish, and seafood.
■ Food bars are potential danger zones. Watch out for fruit ambrosia, puddings, pasta and meat salads, seeds, nuts, and olives.

BONANZA

Best Bets*

Beef
Peppercorn sirloin (6.5 oz.)
Sirloin tips (5 oz.)
Top sirloin (5 oz.)

Chicken
Chicken Monterey breast (6 oz.)
Teriyaki chicken breast (6 oz.)
Honey mustard chicken breast (6 oz.)
Barbecue chicken breast (6 oz.)

Seafood
Charbroiled shrimp
Charbroiled salmon filet (6 oz.)

Sandwiches
Chicken Monterey sandwich (4 oz.)
Homestyle burger (5.5 oz.)

Choose baked potato or rice pilaf as side dish with entrees.

PUTTING IT ALL TOGETHER

Light Choice
(Low in calories, fat, and cholesterol)
Teriyaki chicken breast (6 oz.)
Baked potato (request mustard on size)
Salad bar with low-calorie Italian salad
    dressing, 2 tbsp. (See page 6 for
    salad bar information.)

Nutrition Values:
Calories 611
Carbohydrate (gm.) 75
Protein (gm.) 53
Fat (gm.) 12
% calories from fat 18
Cholesterol (mg.) 110
Sodium (mg.) 1562

Exchanges:
4 Starch/Breads, 4 Meats (lean),
3 Vegetables

Moderate Choice
(Moderate in calories, low in fat, cholesterol)
Sirloin tips, 5 oz.
Baked potato with cottage cheese (2
    tbsp.) from salad bar
Salad bar with French salad dressing
    (2 tbsp.) with additional vinegar or
    lemon wedges (See page 6 for salad
    bar information.)

Nutrition Values:
Calories 783
Carbohydrate (gm.) 79
Protein (gm.) 43
Fat (gm.) 35
% calories from fat 40
Cholesterol (mg.) 97
Sodium (mg.) 1165

Exchanges:
4 Starch/Breads, 4 Meats (medium),
3 Vegetables, 2 Fats

CHART HOUSE

Best Bets

Appetizers
Shrimp cocktail
Spiced shrimp
Oysters on the half shell (6)

Steaks (served with baked potato)
Pepper steak
Top sirloin steak (share)
Teriyaki top sirloin steak (share)

Seafood (served with rice)
Shrimp teriyaki
Australian lobster

Chicken (served with rice)
Teriyaki chicken (request skin removed)

Fresh Vegetables
Baked potato
California artichoke
Chart House rice

Chart House will remove skin from chicken upon request. All entrees served with hot sourdough or squaw (dark) bread, plus New England clam chowder or Chart House salad (choose garden, spinach, or Caesar salad with dressing on side).

PUTTING IT ALL TOGETHER

Light Choice
(Low in calories, fat, and cholesterol)
Oysters on the half shell (6)
   with cocktail sauce
California artichoke (served with
   lemon and 2 tsp. butter)
Chart House rice

Nutrition Values:
Calories 536
Carbohydrate (gm.) 83
Protein (gm.) 26
Fat (gm.) 13
% calories from fat 22
Cholesterol (mg.) 95
Sodium (mg.) 1462

Exchanges:
3 Starch/Breads, 3 Meats (lean),
4 Vegetables, 1 Fat

Moderate Choice
(Moderate in calories, low in fat, cholesterol)
Shrimp teriyaki
Chart House rice
Spinach salad with vinaigrette salad
   dressing, request on side (2 tbsp.)
Beer, light† (12 oz.)

Nutrition Values:
Calories 818
Carbohydrate (gm.) 53
Protein (gm.) 60
Fat (gm.) 30
% calories from fat 33
Cholesterol (mg.) 419*
Sodium (mg.) 1516
   High in cholesterol because of shrimp.
Exchanges:
3 Starch/Breads, 6 Meats (lean)
2 Vegetables, 2 Fats

†Alcohol not accounted for in exchanges.

OUTBACK STEAKHOUSE

Best Bets

Aussie-Tizers
Grilled shrimp on the barbie (hold remoulade sauce)

Land Rovers (request served with house salad, dressing on side, baked jacket potato or fresh steamed veggies)
Victoria's Filet® (9 oz. tenderloin—request to share)

The mustard vinaigrette salad dressing is not low calorie, but contains little olive oil.

Grilled on the Barbie (order house salad, dressing on side with entree)
Chicken on the Barbie, grilled breast (request barbecue sauce on side and fresh veggies)
Botany Bay fish o' the day, grilled (served with fresh veggies)

Sides
Baked jacket potato
Fresh veggies
House or Caesar salad (with dressing on side, hold cheese and croutons)

PUTTING IT ALL TOGETHER

Light Choice
(Low in calories, fat, and cholesterol)
Grilled shrimp on the barbie
Baked jacket potato (hold butter and sour cream)
Fresh veggies
Salad (hold cheese and croutons, request mustard vinaigrette on side)

Nutrition Values:
Calories 464
Carbohydrate (gm.) 53
Protein (gm.) 29
Fat (gm.) 17
% calories from fat 34
Cholesterol (mg.) 153
Sodium (mg.) 1542

Exchanges:
3 Starch/Breads, 2 Meats (lean), 2 Vegetable, 1 Fat

Moderate Choice
(Moderate in calories, low in fat, cholesterol)
Botany Bay fish o' the day (nutrition analysis done with red snapper, 6 oz. portion, cooked)
Fresh veggies
Caesar salad (romaine lettuce, egg, croutons; request dressing on side, 2 tbsp.)
Wine, white* (6 oz.)

Nutrition Values:
Calories 613
Carbohydrate (gm.) 18
Protein (gm.) 52
Fat (gm.) 24
% calories from fat 35
Cholesterol (mg.) 144
Sodium (mg.) 1626

Exchanges:
6 Meats (lean), 3 Vegetables, 1 Fat
Alcohol not accounted for in exchanges.

PONDEROSA

Best Bets

Food bar available —Grand Buffet

Seafood
Baked Scrod (7 oz. cooked)
Broiled halibut, roughy, salmon,
swordfish, or trout (5 to 6 oz. cooked)

Chicken
Grilled chicken breast (5.5 oz.)

Beef
Chopped steak (4 oz.)
Kansas City strip (5 oz.)
Sandwich steak (4 oz.)
Sirloin tips (5 oz.)
Steak kabobs (3 oz.)
Teriyaki steak (5 oz.)

PUTTING IT ALL TOGETHER

Light Choice
(Low in calories, fat, and cholesterol)
Grand Buffet (See page 6 for salad bar
information.)

Nutrition Values:
Calories 551
Carbohydrate (gm.) 84
Protein (gm.) 22
Fat (gm.) 18
% calories from fat 29
Cholesterol (mg.) 39
Sodium (mg.) 1634

Exchanges:
2 Starch/Breads, 2 Meats (medium)
3 Vegetables, 2 Fruits, 2 Fats

Moderate Choice
(Moderate in calories, low in fat, cholesterol)
Steak kabobs
Rice pilaf
Grand Buffet with ranch salad
dressing, 2 tbsp. (See page 6 for salad
bar information.)

Nutrition Values:
Calories 787
Carbohydrate (gm.) 74
Protein (gm.) 42
Fat (gm.) 37
% calories from fat 42
Cholesterol (mg.) 95
Sodium (mg.) 1024

Exchanges:
4 Starch/Breads, 4 Meats (medium),
3 Vegetables, 2 Fats

QUINCY'S FAMILY STEAKHOUSE

Best Bets

Beef
U.S.D.A. choice sirloins
  Petite (5 oz.)
  Filet mignon (7 oz.)
Sirloin tips with peppers and onions
Chopped steak
Quarter pound hamburger with lettuce and tomato

Chicken
Grilled chicken sandwich
Grilled chicken breast (regular size)

Seafood
Grilled trout

Country Sideboard
With entree
Garden salad bar only
Spud 'n salad

Low-fat milk (2%) and low-fat frozen yogurt are available, as well as fresh fruit in the food bar.

PUTTING IT ALL TOGETHER

Light Choice
(Low in calories, fat, and cholesterol)
Spud 'n Salad, salad bar with vinegar and oil (2 tbsp. each on salad). (See page 6 for salad bar information.)

Milk (2%), 8 oz.

Nutrition Values:
Calories 632
Carbohydrate (gm.) 86
Protein (gm.) 23
Fat (gm.) 25
% calories from fat 36
Cholesterol (mg.) 22
Sodium (mg.) 797

Exchanges:
4 Starch/Breads, 3 Vegetables,
1 Milk (2%), 3 Fats

Moderate Choice
(Moderate in calories, low in fat, cholesterol)
Filet mignon, 7 oz.
Baked potato (request lemon wedges)
Salad bar with Thousand Island salad dressing, 2 tbsp. (See page 6 for salad bar information.)
Low-fat frozen yogurt, 6 oz.

Nutrition Values:
Calories 833
Carbohydrate (gm.) 104
Protein (gm.) 58
Fat (gm.) 17
% calories from fat 18
Cholesterol (mg.) 168*
Sodium (mg.) 998
* High in cholesterol.

Exchanges:
5 Starch/Breads, 7 Meats (lean),
3 Vegetables, 1 Fruit

RYAN'S FAMILY STEAK HOUSE

Best Bets

Beef
Petite sirloin
Sirloin tips
Tips (sirloin) with peppers and onions
Tips (sirloin) with mushroom sauce
Filet mignon (5.5 oz.)
Hamburger steak, plain
Hamburger steak with peppers and onions
Hamburger, plain
Steak sandwich

Ryan's Family Steak House offers fat-free salad dressings, nonfat frozen yogurt, Crystal Lite low-calorie beverages, and low-fat milk. Limited information was available on the serving sizes of menu items listed here.

Chicken
Hawaiian chicken, petite
Grilled skinless chicken breast (3 oz. cooked)

Seafood
Salmon, grilled or baked filet
Catch of the day, grilled or baked
Rainbow trout, baked or charbroiled

Soups and Salad
Salad plate, large
Salad (large) with baked potato

Side Orders
Salad plate, small (with entree only)
Garden salad
Baked potato or rice
Peppers and onions

PUTTING IT ALL TOGETHER

Light Choice
(Low in calories, fat, and cholesterol)
Grilled skinless chicken breast
Baked potato (request mustard on side)
Salad bar with low-calorie Italian salad dressing, 2 tbsp. (See page 6 for salad bar information.)
Milk (2%), 8 oz.

Nutrition Values:
Calories 666
Carbohydrate (gm.) 86
Protein (gm.) 48
Fat (gm.) 16
% calories from fat 22
Cholesterol (mg.) 92
Sodium (mg.) 1397

Exchanges:
4 Starch/Breads, 3 Meats (lean)
3 Vegetables, 1 Milk (2%)

Moderate Choice
(Moderate in calories, low in fat, cholesterol)
Grilled salmon, 6 oz. cooked
Rice
Salad bar with low-calorie Italian salad dressing, 2 tbsp. (See page 6 for salad bar information.)
Nonfat frozen yogurt, 6 oz.

Nutrition Values:
Calories 1001
Carbohydrate (gm.) 101
Protein (gm.) 65
Fat (gm.) 37
% calories from fat 33
Cholesterol (mg.) 83
Sodium (mg.) 1085

Exchanges:
4 Starch/Breads, 6 Meats (lean)
3 Vegetables, 2 Fruits, 4 Fats

SIRLOIN STOCKADE

Best Bets

Steaks
Petite sirloin
Kansas City strip
Sirloin tips
Chopped sirloin

Seafood
Catfish filets
Baked cod

Chicken
Chicken breast
Teriyaki breast

Sandwiches
Hamburger
Chicken sandwich

Side Items
Fresh broccoli (hold cheese sauce)
Pasta with marinara sauce

Food bar available. No serving sizes available. Baked potato served with entree.

PUTTING IT ALL TOGETHER

Light Choice
(Low in calories, fat, and cholesterol)
Baked cod, 6 oz. cooked
Baked potato (request 2 tbsp. of sour
   cream on side)
Broccoli (hold cheese sauce, request
   lemon wedges)
Fresh fruit from food bar, 1/2 cup

Nutrition Values:
Calories 511
Carbohydrate (gm.) 55
Protein (gm.) 47
Fat (gm.) 13
% calories from fat 22
Cholesterol (mg.) 106
Sodium (mg.) 727

Exchanges:
3 Starch/Breads, 6 Meats (lean),
1 Vegetable

Moderate Choice
(Moderate in calories, low in fat, cholesterol)
Chopped sirloin, 6 oz.
Pasta with marinara sauce
Salad bar with vinegar as salad
   dressing. (See page 6 for salad
   bar information.)

Nutrition Values:
Calories 824
Carbohydrate (gm.) 86
Protein (gm.) 51
Fat (gm.) 33
% calories from fat 36
Cholesterol (mg.) 171
Sodium (mg.) 1129
High in cholesterol.

Exchanges:
4 Starch/Breads, 4 Meats (medium),
4 Vegetables, 2 Fats

STEAK & ALE

Best Bets

Appetizers
Burgundy mushrooms
Shrimp cocktail

Seafood (includes warm bread, choice of Caesar salad—request dressing on side, or salad bar)
Blackened red snapper (hold butter sauce or serve on side)
Shrimp pilaf
Lobster tails and potato (hold butter sauce or serve on side)

Chicken (includes pilaf, vegetable, warm bread, choice of Caesar salad—with dressing on side, or salad bar)
Blackened chicken breasts, 2 (share)
Blackened chicken pasta
Hawaiian chicken, small

Steaks (choose baked potato, vegetable, warm bread, choice of Caesar salad or salad bar)
Top sirloin, petite (6.75 oz.)
Filet, petite (7 oz.)

PUTTING IT ALL TOGETHER

Light Choice
(Low in calories, fat, and cholesterol)
Jumbo shrimp cocktail with cocktail sauce
Caesar salad (romaine lettuce, egg, bacon, croutons—request dressing on side, 2 tbsp.)
Warm bread (1 slice)

Nutrition Values:
Calories 446
Carbohydrate (gm.) 40
Protein (gm.) 30
Fat (gm.) 18
% calories from fat 36
Cholesterol (mg.) 240
Sodium (mg.) 1445

Exchanges:
2 Starch/Breads
3 Meats (lean)
2 Vegetables
2 Fats

Moderate Choice
(Moderate in calories, low in fat, cholesterol)
Blackened red snapper (with buttery sauce on side or hold)
Rice pilaf
Vegetable (with lemon wedges)
Salad bar with 2 tbsp. ranch salad dressing. (See page 6 for salad bar information.)
Hot apple pie, share (hold ice cream)
Beer, light* (12 oz.)

Nutrition Values:
Calories 1004
Carbohydrate (gm.) 103
Protein (gm.) 64
Fat (gm.) 30
% calories from fat 27
Cholesterol (mg.) 80
Sodium (mg.) 1717

Exchanges:
4 Starch/Breads, 6 Meats (lean)
4 Vegetables, 1 Fruit, 2 Fats
Alcohol not accounted for in exchanges.

STUART ANDERSON'S

Best Bets

Appetizers
Shrimp cocktail with cocktail sauce

Fresh Fish and Seafood
Baked salmon (share)
Fresh fish of the day, lightly grilled
Alaskan crab, 1 pound (share or take
    half home)
Lobster
Grilled prawns

Steaks of the West
Top sirloin, petite cut, 7 oz.
Filet mignon, regular cut, 7.5 oz.
London broil
Teriyaki steak

Chicken
Grilled marinated chicken
Sizzling chicken
Grilled teriyaki chicken (served over
    rice pilaf and pineapple)

Stuart Anderson's dinners include fresh baked bread, all-you-can-eat garden salad, and choice of baked potato, rice pilaf, or fresh steamed vegetable.

PUTTING IT ALL TOGETHER

Light Choice
(Low in calories, fat, and cholesterol)
Sizzling garlic chicken breasts, 2 (with
    sweet peppers and onions, and red
    potatoes; split entree)
Salad bar (order one extra trip to salad
    bar) with French salad dressing, 2
    tbsp. (See page 6 for salad bar
    information.)

Moderate Choice
(Moderate in calories, low in fat, cholesterol)
Shrimp cocktail with cocktail sauce
    (split)
London broil (split and order extra
    potato and extra trip to salad bar)
Salad bar with Thousand Island
    salad dressing, 2 tbsp. (See page 6
    for salad bar information.)

Nutrition Values:
Calories 684
Carbohydrate (gm.) 73
Protein (gm.) 39
Fat (gm.) 29
% calories from fat 38
Cholesterol (mg.) 76
Sodium (mg.) 1591

Exchanges:
3 Starch/Breads, 3 Meats (lean)
4 Vegetables, 4 Fats

Nutrition Values:
Calories 855
Carbohydrate (gm.) 86
Protein (gm.) 51
Fat (gm.) 23
% calories from fat 24
Cholesterol (mg.) 173*
Sodium (mg.) 1363
                                    *High in cholesterol.

Exchanges:
4 Starch/Breads, 5 Meats (lean)
4 Vegetables, 1 Fat

WESTERN SIZZLIN STEAK & MORE

Best Bets

Steak and More
Lean top sirloin
Filet
Chopped sirloin
Sirloin tips

Chicken
Chicken breast dinner (Cajun, teriyaki, or plain)

Seafood
Catch of the day
Grilled catfish

Burgers and More
Hamburger
Chicken breast sandwich (BBQ, Cajun, teriyaki, or plain)

Garden Salad

PUTTING IT ALL TOGETHER

Light Choice
(Low in calories, fat, and cholesterol)
Hamburger on roll with ketchup, 1 tbsp.
Salad bar with lemon wedges (See page 6 for salad bar information.)

Nutrition Values:
Calories 564
Carbohydrate (gm.) 61
Protein (gm.) 32
Fat (gm.) 23
% calories from fat 37
Cholesterol (mg.) 74
Sodium (mg.) 1458

Exchanges:
3 Starch/Breads, 3 Meats (medium), 3 Vegetables, 1 Fat

Moderate Choice
(Moderate in calories, low in fat, cholesterol)
Cajun chicken breast sandwich on roll
Salad bar with 2 tbsp blue cheese dressing (See page 6 for salad bar information.)
Fresh melon and pineapple from salad bar (1 cup)

Nutrition Values:
Calories 713
Carbohydrate (gm.) 64
Protein (gm.) 49
Fat (gm.) 30
% of calories from fat 38
Cholesterol (mg.) 101
Sodium (mg.) 1748

Exchanges:
2 Starch/Bread, 5 Meats (lean), 3 Vegetables, 1 Fruit, 3 Fats

ALPHABETICAL LISTING OF RESTAURANTS IN THIS BOOK

CHRONIMED Publishing
Books of Related Interest

The Healthy Eater's Guide to Family & Chain Restaurants by Hope S. Warshaw, M.M.Sc., R.D. Here's the only guide that tells you how to eat healthier in over 100 of America's most popular family and chain restaurants. It offers complete and up-to-date nutrition information and suggests which items to choose and avoid.

004214,   ISBN 1-56561-017-2 $9.95

Fast Food Facts by Marion Franz, R.D., M.S. This revised and up-to-date best-seller shows how to make smart nutrition choices at fast food restaurants—and tells what to avoid. Includes complete nutrition information on more than 1,000 menu offerings from the 21 largest fast food chains.

Standard-size edition   004068,   ISBN 0-937721-67-0 $6.95
Pocket edition   004073,   ISBN 0-937721-69-7 $4.95

Convenience Food Facts by Arlene Monk, R.D., C.D.E., with Marion Franz, R.D., M.S. C.D.E. Includes complete nutrition information, tips, and exchange values on more than 1,500 popular name-brand processed foods commonly found in grocery store freezers and shelves. Helps you plan easy-to-prepare, nutritious meals.

004081,   ISBN 0-937721-77-8$10.95

The Label Reader's Pocket Dictionary of Food Additives by Mike Lapchick with Cindy Appleseth, R.Ph., is the only quick-reference guide to more than 250 of today's most common food additives– found in virtually everything we eat. It has the latest findings in an easy-to-read dictionary format with all the information you'll need to make intelligent food decisions.

004224,   ISBN 1-56561-027-X $4.95

Exchanges for All Occasions by Marion Franz, R.D., M.S. Exchanges and meal planning suggestions for just about any occasion, sample meal plans, special tips for people with diabetes, and more.

004003,   ISBN 0-937721-22-0$12.95

Fight Fat & Win by Elaine Moquette-Magee, R.D., M.P.H. This breakthrough book explains how to easily incorporate low-fat dietary guidelines into every modern eating experience, from fast-food and common restaurants to quick meals at home, simply by making smarter choices.

004070,   ISBN 0-937721-65-4 $9.95

One Year of Healthy, Hearty, and Quick One-Dish Meals by Pam Spaude and Jan Owan-McMenamin, R.D., is a collection of 365 easy-to-make healthy and tasty family favorites and unique creations that are meals in themselves. Most of the dishes take under 30 minutes to prepare.

004217,   ISBN 1-56561-019-9$12.95

Let Them Eat Cake by Virginia N. White with Rosa A. Mo, R.D. If you're looking for delicious and healthy pies, cookies, puddings, and cakes, this book will give you your just desserts. With easy, step-by-step instructions, this innovative cookbook features complete nutrition information, the latest exchange values, and tips on making your favorite snacks more healthful.

004206,   ISBN 1-56561-011-3$12.95

Beyond Alfalfa Sprouts and Cheese: The Healthy Meatless Cookbook by Judy Gilliard and Joy Kirkpatrick, R.D., includes creative and savory meatless dishes using ingredients found in just about every grocery store. It also contains helpful cooking tips, complete nutrition information, and the latest exchange values.

004218,   ISBN 1-56561-020-2$12.95

60 Days of Low-Fat, Low-Cost Meals in Minutes by M.J. Smith, R.D., L.D., M.A. Following the path of the best-seller *All American Low-Fat Meals in Minutes,* here are more than 150 quick and sumptuous recipes complete with the latest exchange values and nutrition facts for lowering calories, fat, salt, and cholesterol. This book contains complete menus for 60 days and recipes that use only ingredients found in virtually any grocery store—most for a total cost of less than $10.

004205,   ISBN 1-56561-010-5$12.95

All-American Low-Fat Meals in Minutes by M.J. Smith, M.A., R.D., L.D. Filled with tantalizing recipes and valuable tips, this cookbook makes great-tasting low-fat foods a snap for holidays, special occasions, or everyday. Most recipes take only minutes to prepare.

004079, ISBN 0-937721-73-5 $12.95

The Guiltless Gourmet by Judy Gilliard and Joy Kirkpatrick, R.D. A perfect fusion of sound nutrition and creative cooking, this book is loaded with delicious recipes high in flavor and low in fat, sugar, calories, cholesterol, and salt.

004021, ISBN 0-937721-23-9 $9.95

The Guiltless Gourmet Goes Ethnic by Judy Gilliard and Joy Kirkpatrick, R.D. More than a cookbook, this sequel to *The Guiltless Gourmet* shows how easy it is to lower the sugar, calories, sodium, and fat in your favorite ethnic dishes—without sacrificing taste.

004072, ISBN 0-937721-68-9 $11.95

European Cuisine from the Guiltless Gourmet by Judy Gilliard and Joy Kirkpatrick, R.D. This book shows you how to lower the sugar, salt, cholesterol, total fat, and calories in delicious Greek, English, German, Russian, and Scandinavian dishes. Plus it features complete nutrition information and the latest exchange values.

004085, ISBN 0-937721-81-6 $11.95

The Joy of Snacks by Nancy Cooper, R.D. Offers more than 200 delicious recipes and nutrition information for hearty snacks, including sandwiches, appetizers, soups, spreads, cookies, muffins, and treats especially for kids. The book also suggests guidelines for selecting convenience snacks and interpreting information on food labels.

004086, ISBN 0-937721-82-4 $12.95

Buy Them at Your Local Bookstore
or
Turn Page for Order Information!

CHRONIMED Publishing
P.O. Box 47945
Minneapolis, MN 55447-9727

Place a check mark next to the book (s) you would like sent. Enclosed is $_____. (Please add $3.00 to this order to cover postage and handling. Minnesota residents add 6.5% sales tax.) Send check or money order, no cash or C.O.D.'s. Prices are subject to change without notice.

Name _____

Address _____

City _____ State_____ Zip_____

Allow 4 to 6 weeks for delivery.
Quantity discounts available upon request.

Or order by phone: 1-800-848-2793,
1-800-444-5951 (non-metro area of Minnesota)
612-546-1146 (Minneapolis/St. Paul metro area).
Please have your credit card number ready.